RIP UP!

RIP UP!

GET ROCK HARD AND SUPER CUT NOW!

ROBERT KENNEDY

Sterling Publishing Co., Inc. New York

Acknowledgments

This book is written to inform, inspire, and educate you about the fine art of ripping up the body. Enjoy it. Few books are the result of just one person's efforts. I owe a debt of appreciation to the various photographers who have contributed pictures to make this volume rich with visual excitement. They include Steve Douglas, Paula Crane, Art Zeller, Bill Heimanson, Doris Barrilleaux, Chris Lund, Denie Walter, Garry Bartlett, Walt Sorenson, Robert Nailon, Doug White, Al Antuck, Bob Gruskin, John Campos, Jim Marchand, Monty Heron, Tapio Hautala, Bob Flippin, Peter Potter, Edward Hankey, John Balik, Mike Neveaux, Reg Bradford, Wayne Gallasch, Paul Goode, Ken Korentayer, Glenn Low, Lou Parees, Roger Shelley, Bill Reynolds, Russ Warner, Eric Chapman, George Greenwood, Joe Valdez, and my custom photoprocessor, Mike Read.

*I would like to thank Ben and Joe Weider, who, in their individual ways, promote the sport of bodybuilding with a degree of competence seldom equalled. Ben, from his offices in Montreal, is constantly building and promoting the International Federation of Bodybuilders (IFBB) and seeking Olympic recognition. Joe, from the other side of the North American continent, heads the amazing Weider Magazine publishing empire. Its periodicals—*Flex, Men's Fitness, Shape, *and* Muscle and Fitness*—consistently herald the bodybuilding way of life. Both men have kept bodybuilding in a high-profile position for many years now. Each is appreciated, for without them the sport would not exist as it does today.*

I would also like to thank Gold's and World's gyms. Both make my photographers welcome whenever a champion bodybuilder has a photo session.

To Sterling Publishing Co., Inc., I offer my gratitude. Their efforts have lead to my selling over one million copies of books promoting the subject of bodybuilding.

Sincere thanks to my ever alert editor Carol Palmer, who keeps my writing lean and readable, and to layout designer Jim Anderson, whose graphic art skills create such a handsome publication. Thank you one and all!

Edited by Carol Palmer
Designed by Jim Anderson

Library of Congress Cataloging-in-Publication Data

Kennedy, Robert, 1938–
Rip up! : get rock hard and super cut now! / by Robert Kennedy.
p. cm.
Includes index.
ISBN 0-8069-6423-5 (pbk.)
1. Bodybuilding I. Title.
GV546.5.K4625 1988 88-20062
646.7'5—dc19 CIP

Published by Sterling Publishing Co., Inc.
Two Park Avenue, New York, N.Y. 10016
Distributed in Canada by Oak Tree Press Ltd.
℅ Canadian Manda Group, P.O. Box 920, Station U
Toronto, Ontario, Canada M8Z 5P9
Distributed in Great Britain and Europe by Cassell PLC
Artillery House, Artillery Row, London SW1P 1RT, England
Distributed in Australia by Capricorn Ltd.
P.O. Box 665, Lane Cove, NSW 2066
Manufactured in the United States of America

Sterling ISBN 0-8069-6423-5 Paper

Contents

The super-striated chest of John Terilli.

Introduction

Ripped! Super-defined, striated, shredded, vascular and cut to the bone! Today's bodybuilding demands more than pure bulk and mass. It demands that physical condition called being ripped where the body has been almost entirely stripped of fat. Being ripped makes the muscles and veins stand out incredibly. Today, it's an absolute essential when competing. You must be cut to the bone to succeed in a bodybuilding contest.

Tom Platz is famous for his huge, super-defined thighs and quadriceps. Bodybuilding pros Gary Strydom, John Hnatyshak, and Lee Haney are among those known for achieving this ripped-up look. Women stars such as Bev Francis, Anja Langer, and Marjo Selin all prove that women will not be left behind in the trend. Women *can* get ripped—in fact, they achieve this look more frequently than their male counterparts despite having higher body fat levels than men.

Vince Gironda was one of the first bodybuilders to achieve the ripped look, but he was not accepted. In fact his vascularity and advanced muscularity were termed "obscene." Today, in the shape he had in the 1950s, Vince would be winning titles.

Clarence Bass was one of the first people to coin the phrase "ripped." The word became synonymous with Bass, a former weightlifter turned bodybuilder.

Clarence Bass coined the phrase "ripped."

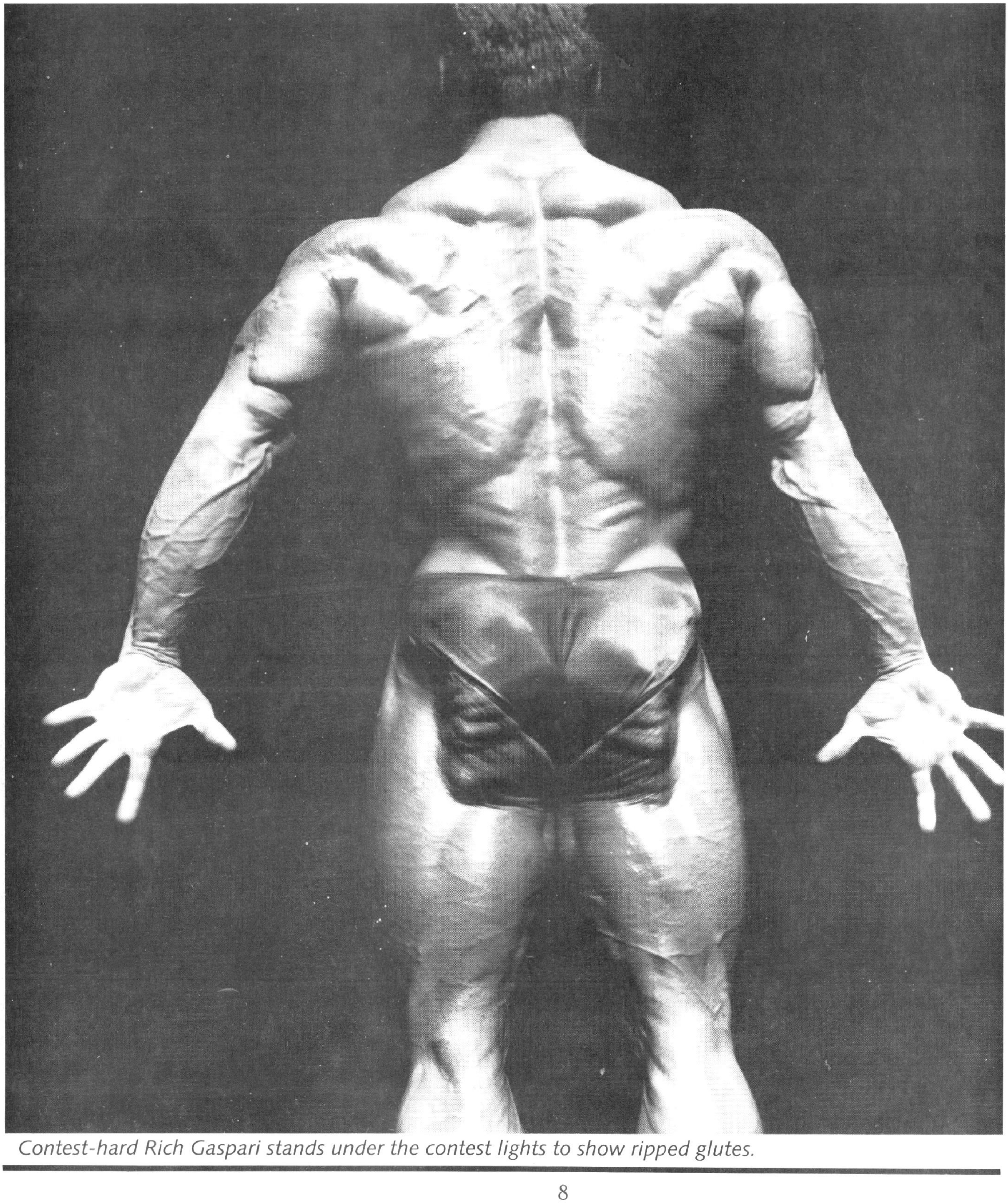

Contest-hard Rich Gaspari stands under the contest lights to show ripped glutes.

Clarence is not genetically perfect for bodybuilding, having a shallow chest and small skeletal structure, but for a person who only turned to bodybuilding in his thirties, he is very well built. He gave new meaning to the word ripped. Like Gary Strydom, Clarence Bass has the super abdominals and intercostals which are the true hallmark of the bodybuilder in top condition.

Rich Gaspari is another bodybuilder noted for his super-striated contest condition. Rich was one of the first to exhibit ripped glutes. Now most bodybuilders are trying to attain this condition.

The ripped look took over in the middle 1970s as a backlash to the bulk craze where everyone was seeking (and many were achieving) 20-inch-plus arms. Frank Zane was the first successful bodybuilder to shed his mass in favor of the ripped physique, which has the benefit of making one appear bigger than fellow competitors with larger measurements. After Zane garnered three Mr. Olympia titles, smaller but ripped bodybuilders like Chris Dickerson and Mohamed Makkawy won a host of contests. Starting with Al Beckles, the bodybuilding world was treated to winners who were not only ripped, but big as well: a double whammy! Today we have Rich Gaspari, Cory Everson, and the amazing Lee Haney, all of whom are ripped and have the advantage of being big and shapely. Will we return to the bulk craze and forsake cuts? It's doubtful.

Some bodybuilders regret that the ripped look ever came in. Their reasoning is that they feel a bodybuilder can be *too* defined. Of course, their opinion is partly based on the fact that ripping up is so difficult to achieve, and therefore, foreseeing their failure to reach the

John Hnatyschak

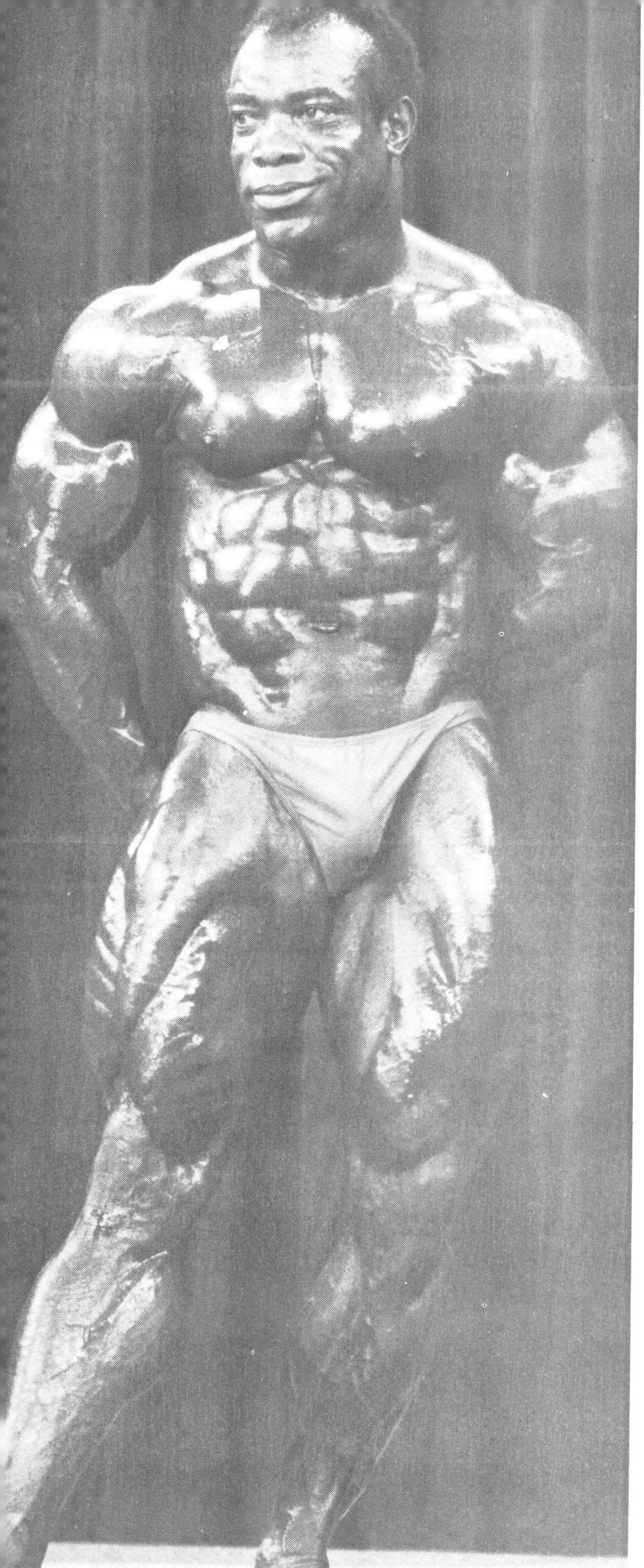

Johnny Fuller is one of the most defined men in the sport.

shredded state, they resort to knocking the concept as being less than ideal.

You don't have to be a pro to be ripped. You, too, can look defined and cut. You can appear stronger, more fit and bigger. Your muscles can take on that whipcord appearance one associates with a construction worker. Getting ripped comes about from concentrated training and from following a calorie-reduced diet. You can achieve this condition by carefully following the instructions in this book.

Understand, though, that few bodybuilders are ripped all the time. It is a difficult, long-fought and hard-won effort that is only achieved by the most dedicated. Pro bodybuilders are shredded for only the few days surrounding the contest, and the timing is so crucial that only a handful of the contestants at a show will be in super-ripped condition. And pros give themselves an off-season after months of rigorously keeping in shape for competition and seminars.

However, *Rip Up!* will not only show you how to get contest-ready, but will also *show you how to achieve a semi-ripped state and hold onto it for as long as you wish.* With diligence and stickability the ordinary person *can* change their body-fat-to-muscle ratio to look muscular and defined *all the time.* When you are ripped you look totally different from the way you look in the so-called off-season. You look and feel great. There's a sense of accomplishment and pride. Tie in this lean look with a healthy-looking tan, maybe a new hairstyle and new set of clothes, and you'll feel on top of the world.

This book is designed for the "fit but smooth" segment of our populace. The Western world is full of fitness enthusiasts, bodybuilders and competitive

Cory Everson and Ellen Van Maris of Holland hit chest poses for the judges.

Larry Scott and Tom Platz are always in great shape.

strength athletes, but sad to say very few look the part. Many bodybuilders *never* get ripped. There are numerous half-hearted attempts but seldom is even the smallest amount of muscular definition achieved. Why do so many men and women who train regularly using aerobics, weights, or resistance machines fail to look physically impressive? Much of it may be due to self image (the way we view ourselves) and deportment (the posture of the body) but in my experience the main reason why so may dedicated bodybuilders and fitness fiends look quite unimpressive in or out of clothes, is that they have spoiled their shape by carrying too high a percentage of body fat.

This is the secret of ripping up: you can do 400-lb. bench presses and 100-lb. concentration curls forever without getting ripped, if your body-fat-to-lean-muscle ratio is too high. *Even if you are not overweight, your body fat percentage will normally be too high to get cut.* Lean and fit men usually have a body fat percentage of 12–16, fit women 22–26. During bodybuilding competition the male pros have a percentage range of 6–10, and the women 10–12—half their normal range. You must build your muscle mass with weight training, and define your muscles by eating a strict, specialized diet. It's that simple. The goals, training and diet rules are the same for men *and* women. You provide the determination, and *Rip Up!* will provide the know-how in detail.

Cutting up the body takes time. You cannot successfully rush the process. You have to set your goal, make your plan, and follow through to the letter. Using this book you can choose to sustain a lean, semi-ripped look or you can pick a date and get contest-hard for a show.

Multi-Mr. Olympia Lee Haney sets the standards for today's competition.

Where to Train

John Hnatyschak

If you're serious about building your body, really serious, then make sure that if you are going to fork out for a gym membership you invest in the right kind of gym. Chrome weights and apparatus, plush, thick-pile carpets and Beethoven's Fifth are not for you. A rugged physique only grows out of a hardcore environment. True bodybuilders detest walking knee-deep in luxurious carpet while trying to exercise.

You may think that a barbell is a barbell, a hack squat machine a hack squat machine, or even that a gym is a gym. Nonsense: In bodybuilding there is *good* apparatus and *bad* apparatus. Chrome weights feel "dead" to the touch . . . and highly chromed machines are invariably designed for looks as opposed to being functional. As for Beethoven, that's listening music, not working-out music.

Spend time in the wrong training environment and you will waste your time. You will not achieve greatness. Whether you train in a home gym or at a commercial establishment, the requirements are the same. The apparatus should be efficient and the atmosphere should be conducive to concentrated hard work without interruption. It's true that an amazing amount of progress can be made with just dumbbells and barbells, a simple bench and support stands, but advanced trainers will require the use of a lat machine, a hack squat apparatus and a thigh extension/thigh curl machine in addition. Other important, though perhaps not as vital, pieces of apparatus include a chin bar, a leg press machine, a preacher bench and a Roman chair sit-up bench.

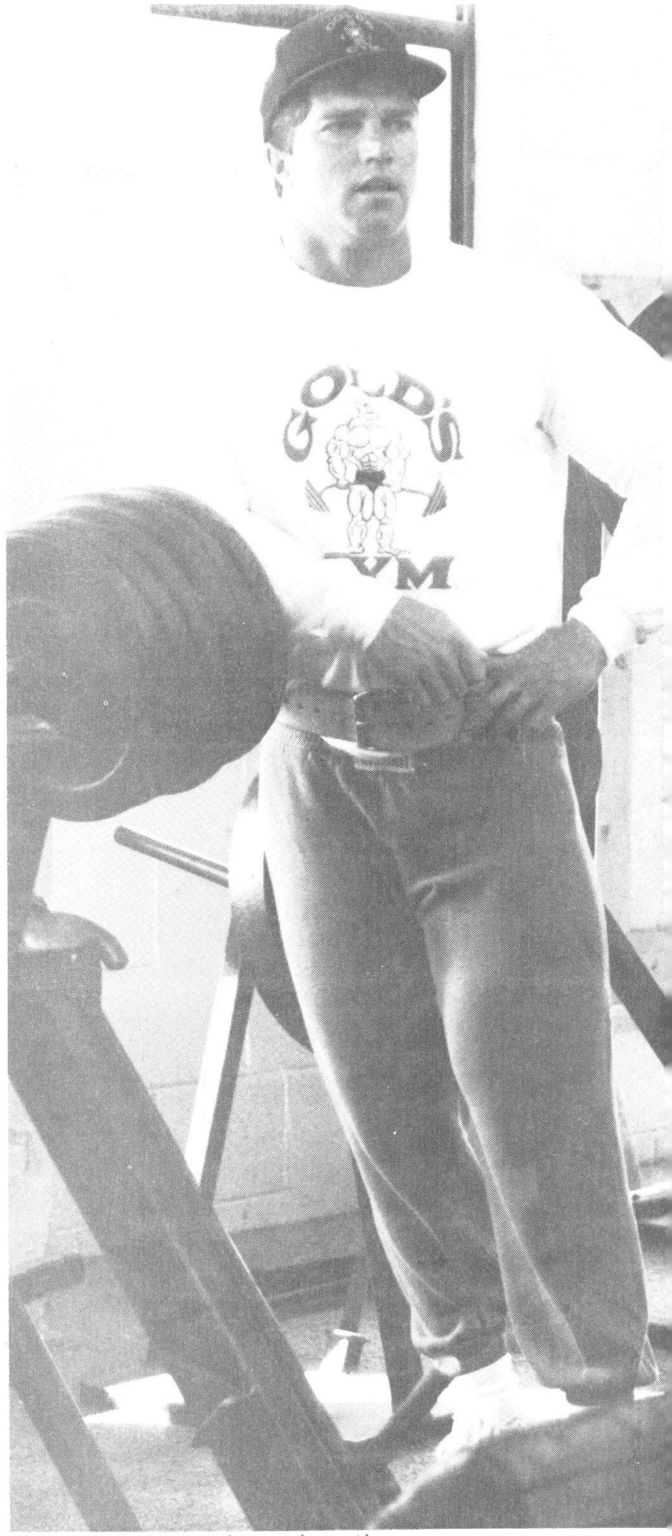

Gary Strydom takes a breather between sets.

Hnatyschak curls.

Home Training

Not all of us can afford a spacious home training area, but obviously a room that allows you to move freely during your training is better than one that is cramped. Natural light is important too, though not essential. What is vital to my mind is the need for mirrors; the more the better. Most home trainers exercise alone, and when you have mirrors reflecting your own image, it like having a training partner. You're inspired to work harder and faster.

The bare-minimum equipment needed in a home gym environment is an adjustable bench, a pair of squat stands, and sufficient free weights to meet your strength needs in the heaviest exercises. The advantages of a home gym are that you can train whenever you want. There is no lining up to use the machines, and you will not be engaged in idle conversation by strangers. Neither will bad weather or national holidays cause you to miss a workout. The two things against home training are that you seldom have access to the variety of apparatus you will find in a commercial gymnasium, and that you could get lazy, knowing that you can train anytime. You might give over your time to eating, watching TV or socializing . . . after which you would be too pooped to work out.

Dumbbell shrugs, Hnatyschak style.

One of the most famous gyms in the world: Gold's Gym, the mecca of bodybuilding.

Bodybuilding Gyms

Most people train harder at bodybuilding gyms such as Gold's or World's because there is invariably a larger variety of apparatus than you will find in a home gym. This keeps boredom at bay.

A hardcore gym, unlike a spa gymnasium, only contains workable tried-and-tested apparatus. There are no toning machines, exercise tables or electronic gismos. A hardcore gym will contain Olympic weights, fixed dumbbells up to 150 lbs., flat benches, squat racks, lat machines, hack lift units, leg curl and thigh extension apparatus, plus a variety of well-made units such as the T-bar row apparatus, calf machines, Roman chairs, chin bars, pek decks, incline, decline and curling benches to enable you to hit different angles.

Since there are more people around you will find yourself training harder than you would at home. Not only is there a mildly competitive atmosphere but there is also the show-off instinct that can

Jon Jon Park, Robert Kennedy, and Gary Strydom.

force us to drum up a little more effort. Finally, exercising with people of the opposite sex can subconsciously stir up the old hormones, which can encourage us to train even harder. Home gym training is fine for people who just want to achieve average results, but if you are aiming for the top then the hardcore bodybuilding gym is the way to go. A handful of champion bodybuilders have home gyms, including Dennis Tinerino, Lee Haney, Frank Zane, Candy Csencsits, and Franco Columbu. But, when competition time comes around, these same champs leave their home gyms and return to the bodybuilding gyms so that they can maximize their efforts. Super competitors only achieve greatness training at hardcore gymnasiums.

Personal Trainers and Training Partners

Some neophyte bodybuilders pay for the services of a personal trainer who puts them through each set in a one-on-one basis. If you are serious about maximizing your progress, this is not a good idea. Many personal trainers have no idea how an aspiring bodybuilder should train and just have general fitness as their goal. When you hire the services of someone to guide you through a workout, you are giving away too much of the responsibility. You lose touch with your body's feedback mechanism. Only *you* know when you're ready for your next set. Only *you* know when a weight should be increased or decreased. Only *you* know when forced reps are required or not required.

Instead of using a personal trainer it is far better and much cheaper to find a workout partner who is actively seeking the same goals as yourself. Train *together*; alternate sets and compete in number of reps performed or poundage used. Your workout partner will pace your training perfectly and the results will astound both of you.

Heavy squats often need the help of a training partner.

Training for Mass with Cuts

Janice Ragain

You have to build your muscles before you can cut 'em, so the foundation of the *Rip Up!* program is progressive weight resistance. I have written hundreds of thousands of words on training and have devoted a whole book to exploring a variety of routines (*Reps!*, Sterling Publishing Co., Inc., New York) to help bodybuilders and fitness advocates reach their best condition ever. As you know, there are numerous principles and systems associated with bodybuilding. This chapter covers principles developed over the years that I feel are the best suited for the quest for a super-cut physique.

A commonly raised point concerning training for definition surrounds the differences in working for cuts versus working for mass. Are there differences? Many bodybuilders feel that the only required change in training for that ripped appearance is dietary: You take in fewer calories. Admittedly, many bodybuilders do get into contest condition by changing nothing about their training, and only make adjustments to their nutrition and supplement intake. But the more sophisticated trainer knows that there is more to it. There are added dimensions which will speed you towards contest shape—factors that will also put you a notch or two ahead of the pack—and they're all listed here.

Gary Strydom

To Start

Always make sure that whenever you start a new exercise program or diet that you are physically suited to the program. It is always a good idea to check with your doctor before forcing drastic change on your system. Are you over 40? Do you have any organ or circulatory disorders? Do you smoke? Have you been inactive for a number of years? Your doctor will want to know the answers. Check yourself out. Chances are you will be given the green light to start the program, but it is always best to double-check with a qualified medical doctor so that you can proceed with confidence. In the unlikely event that you do have some kind of disorder, then all the more reason to be happy that you consulted your MD. Steps can be taken to correct the problem and advice will be given so that you can tailor your own program according to your individual level of health and capacity for vigorous exercise.

When you embark on a program to sharpen and rip up your physique, you will have to involve yourself in a new "mind-set." You must take time to mentally resolve to achieve your training goal. Things are often made easier if you have a contest date to aim for. If you want a maintainable look, you should still set a date to achieve the semi-ripped look by, and use this date as a "countdown." It's the best method to push yourself and ensure success.

The Ripping Up Workout

When you are ripping up, the workout has to serve several needs at one and the same time: mass-building through weight resistance, adjusting the metabolism through aerobics for improved fat-burning, and training for cuts and definition. Keep these points in mind when you train:

- Your workout must contain *some* very intense training (forced reps) for hard-to-build areas because as we diet down, muscle size is invariably lost in our weakest (hardest to build) muscle groups. High-intensity work will help us keep muscle mass, as a strict diet frequently robs us of some muscle size.
- Increase training frequency. Most bodybuilders gain mass most efficiently when training each body part twice weekly. Those wishing to cut up the physique may benefit from a limited period of increasing workouts to the extent where they are training each body area up to three times per week.
- Workouts, in addition to being more frequent than in off-season training, should be performed at a brisker pace, with many exercises using higher reps, to create a fat-burning effect that will better guarantee the chance of achieving a hundred-percent-ripped condition.
- Cut down on your resting time between sets of each exercise. Do not wait until your breathing rate returns to normal.
- As a general rule, use higher repetitions when training for cuts. The aerobic effect is increased and more blood is forced into the muscle.
- Use less weight when training to get ripped. Your job is to make the muscles *feel* the stress, not to demonstrate your strength ability to other gym members.
- Switch over to using dumbbells instead of barbells for the majority of your exercises. Dumbbells force each arm to

Incline dumbbell flyes as demonstrated by Serge Nubret.

work independently, and, consequently, slightly more effort is needed when using dumbbells. Also, you are "hitting" your muscles from a different angle.

- Do not lock-out on your exercises. Stop each repetition just short of locking out the arms or legs. This will keep pressure on the muscles as well as safeguarding the joints from injury.

Pushing for pec development: Gary Strydom.

- Use strict form. Reduce all bouncing and swinging of the weights. Focus on making the exercise harder rather than easier. Control the resistance entirely.
- Do not allow your concentration to break when you are trying to rip up the physique. Concentrate on every part of each rep. Place your mind inside the muscle and *think* power and impressiveness.
- Use a greater proportion of isolation exercises than when training for mass. Make good use of movements such as concentration curls, triceps extensions, leg curls, the pec-deck machine, thigh extensions, and lateral raises.
- Use isotension: squeeze the bars and flex the muscles being worked as each repetition is concluded to increase the intensity.
- Aerobic exercise is better than weight-lifting when it comes to burning off calories. Incorporate some aerobic exercise in your overall program. The stationary bike, low-impact jogging, or fast walking two or three times a week are great fat-burning movements that will help rid the body of excess adipose tissue. Plus, your metabolism will change to become more efficient.
- The new concept to finishing off the physique is called *flex-posing*. After each workout flex each muscle six times, and on the final repetition, hold for a count of ten. Flex-posing is not the same as posing for competition. It is the systematic flexing of individual muscles whether or not they are posed in a traditional stance. There's a bonus to being ripped. When you are ripped, not only do your muscles "pop out" incredibly, but you will find that you will also be able to flex and control them more easily during your posing routine.

Training Techniques

Straight Sets

Straight sets are the most common and effective form of training for bodybuilders at all levels of experience.

A straight set is a series of repetitions of an exercise performed continuously until the last rep is completed. After this there is a pause or short rest (usually 30–90 seconds) and then a second set of reps is performed. For example, a routine can ask for "3 sets of 6 reps." Those who use many sets involve more and more muscle fibres with every set performed, and typically a serious bodybuilder will perform 3–6 sets per exercise, sometimes more.

1

2

3

E-Z bar curls by Bill Grant, who is famous for his mountainous biceps development.

4

A large percentage of bodybuilders lack confidence when it comes to increasing weight on dumbbells, barbells and exercise machines. Once they get to a certain weight resistance, they are frequently loath to push beyond to a stage where the intensity factor is raised to an uncomfortable zone. It is a good idea to raise the weight used whenever you feel you can handle more. Don't wait for your current poundages to "feel light." It may never happen. Rather, you should grab the opportunity to add resistance when you feel it is within your ability, always being aware that strict form and the use of isotension are important.

On the other hand, if you can't keep strict form on an exercise, you are probably being too ambitious about how much weight you can handle and may be setting yourself up for an injury.

Awesome is the only word for Gary Strydom.

Priority Training

It's generally accepted that we all have more energy at the beginning of a workout than at the end. Some bodybuilders pace themselves well during their workouts so that they can do justice to every exercise, but even so, the exercises they do at the beginning of their routine get the lion's share of the available energy.

The muscle priority system is a method by which you train your most underdeveloped body part *first* in the routine, at a time when both your energy and enthusiasm are at a peak. This works particularly well with those who have weak abdominals or thighs (typically under par areas). By working them first when energy is high, they get plenty of quality work.

Super Sets

This method involves the use of two exercises, each alternated with the other with no rest between sets. The idea behind the concept is to alternate a particular muscle with its opposite counterpart. For example, a typical superset would involve one set of biceps training with one set of triceps training. Other typical supersets would consist of alternating chins for the back with bench presses for the chest, or alternating thigh extensions for the quads with thigh curls for the hamstrings.

The advantage of supersets is that one can pump up an area such as the arms in double-quick time. A great deal of work can be achieved in a short period of time. The disadvantage is that because no rest is taken between sets, slightly less weight is used in the actual exercises. Supersets, however, are used

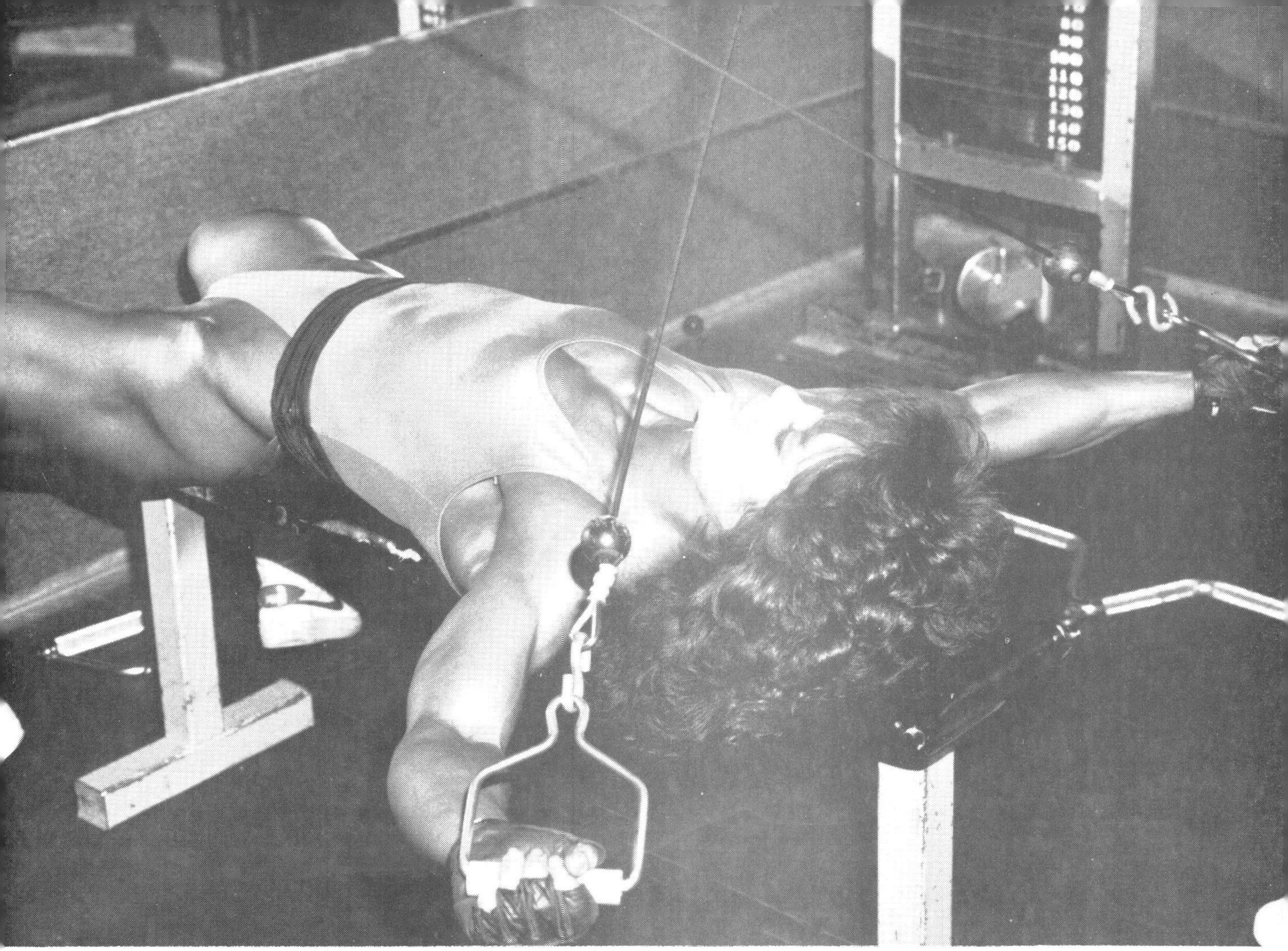

Claire Furr works her rear deltoids with cable flat-bench flyes.

extensively by those preparing for a contest.

Continuous Tension

This is a training practice whereby you maintain the stress of the resistance throughout the range of motion. You can maintain tension by slowing up the exercise when a repetition gets easy. Continuous tension can also be produced by isotension: deliberately tensing a muscle while exercising.

Those training in the final stages of precontest preparation may find particular value in combining continuous tension with peak contraction, explained on p. 31. In this way, ultimate detail and separation will appear in your muscles as the contest date approaches, always assuming that superfluous fat is removed from under the skin by a strict calorie-controlled diet.

The most common method of applying continuous tension to your training is to avoid locking any joints during your exercises. Locked elbows or knee joints usually, though not always, constitute relief from muscle tension. Avoid doing this in squats, presses, chins, curls, supine presses, triceps extensions, thigh curls, dips, incline presses—and you will bring continuous tension into play.

Compound Sets

This system is also known as giant sets. It is an advanced technique that is used by many top bodybuilders at times during their training.

Select four or five exercises for a particular muscle group and perform each consecutively, one after the other, with no more rest than it takes to walk to the next station and start exercising. After completing one set each of your chosen exercises, take a short breather and then run through all the exercises again. As an example of a compound set study the following suggestion for an entire chest routine. Each compound set is performed three times.

Compound Set		Reps
Bench Press with Dumbbells	×	10
Incline, Dumbbell Bench Press	×	10
Flat Bench Flye	×	10
Cable Crossover	×	12
Rest (two minutes)		

The following is a compound set for the biceps (performed three times).

Compound Set		Reps
Barbell Curl	×	8
Incline Dumbbell Curl (40° incline)	×	10
Preacher Bench Curl (barbell)	×	10
Seated Hammer Curl	×	12

Bob Jodkiewicz demonstrates incline dumbbell curls.

T-bar row by Bob Jodkiewicz: start.

Rest-Pause Sets

The renewed popularity of the rest-pause system was brought about by one man: Mike Mentzer. "Rest-pause training is the most advanced, intensive, stressful form of training to date. Its effects are immediate and very dramatic," he said. Actually, Mentzer cautions against overtraining when using the rest-pause method. Beginners and intermediates would be well advised not to use the principle until they get into more advanced training.

Let's use the Universal bench press apparatus to illustrate rest-pause training. Select a weight in which you can perform only one repetition. After you have completed the single rep, rest for 10–15 seconds (to recover strength). Complete another repetition with the same weight followed by another rest of 10–15 seconds. Do this for five to eight reps. You may require that your training partner decrease the weight resistance slightly after three or four reps, which is normal.

Rest-pause training works best with large muscle groups, especially those exercises involving multi-joint action. It can, however, be used with any exercise. If free weights are used, they have to

T-bar row: finish.

1

2

Ali Mala: lateral raises.

3

be returned to the rack (in the case of squats, bench presses, dumbbell presses, dumbbell curls, etc.) between repetitions. In the case of barbell exercises, you could return the bar to a bench to avoid having to pick it up from the floor between rest-pause repetitions.

Up-and-Down-The-Rack Sets

Vince Gironda has been using this method now for over fifty years. His famous pupil Larry Scott uses it extensively for shoulder training and even today, in his fifties, Scott has phenomenal deltoid development.

Here's how the method works: Stand near a dumbbell rack and curl the 20-pound dumbbells (or another low weight to begin with) five reps. Move up to the 25-pounders for five reps and then to the 30-pounders, the 35-pounders, and so on, up the rack. Advanced men will go up to 70- or 80-pound dumbbells; women may only be able to use 40-pound dumbbells. The point is to go as heavy as you can while still performing four or five repetitions. After you reach your limit, decrease the poundage, still using the same number of repetitions, making sure that you take no more than a five- or ten-second rest between each set. Obviously, you need a set-up rack to follow this method. It would be pointless to use one pair of dumbbells for this training procedure because far too much time would be taken to change the weights.

Peak Contraction

Muscle contraction *is* bodybuilding, and the peak contraction principle is a method of maximizing the amount of muscle fibres used during exercise.

Peak contraction can be defined as a movement in which a muscle is stressed to its maximum at the *conclusion* of the repetition. For example, the regular barbell curl in which the barbell passes through the most difficult part of the exercise when the lower arms are parallel to the floor, is *not* a peak contraction since there is a definite easing of resistance as the bar reaches the shoulders. In fact, most exercises get easier as each rep is concluded.

A peak contraction occurs at a time when you are contracted to the limit, and the particular exercise or the machine being used will not let you work or move beyond this contraction. Pure peak contraction movements include wide-grip upright rows, wide-grip lat-machine pulldowns, triceps kickbacks, standing leg curls, wide-grip bent-over rows, wide-grip chins, 90° preacher bench curls, crunches, gravity-boot sit-ups, thigh extensions, and incline triceps stretches. There are scores of exercises that can be altered to peak contraction simply by altering angles of benches, pulleys and weights in relation to your body. For ex-

Thigh extensions by world champ Bev Francis.

Massive Australian Bev Francis.

ample, Vince Gironda turns a calf raise into a peak-contraction exercise by having his students face the opposite way towards the machine on a hack machine, holding the slide handles while performing heel raises. By using a lat machine, and lying under it in a supine position (on your back) you can do a useful peak-contraction pulley curl.

Few training methods make more use of the mind than peak contraction movements. You need pinpoint concentration at the conclusion of each repetition when the maximum number of nerve impulses are being fired by the muscle.

"My recommendation," says Mike Mentzer, "is that at least one exercise for each muscle group should provide a strong resistance in the contracted position."

Advanced bodybuilders who use peak contractions in some of their exercises agree that the muscles must tense and contract beyond what is imposed by the resistance. In other words, you must consciously squeeze and tense them to their fullest at the conclusion of each peak contraction.

Pre-Exhaust Technique

Many people are aware of the fact that I invented the pre-exhaust technique. Today, pre-exhaust is a very popular method of exercising. The original theory was materialized out of necessity, for I desperately wanted to widen my shoulders. Although I had performed thousands of sets of presses in all the barbell and dumbbell variations, and duly followed these heavy sets with a variety of dumbbell laterals, workout after workout, I just could not work my shoulders hard enough to make them sore the next day, which would indicate muscle growth. I clearly defined the problem as needing to work the deltoid cap more vigorously than it had ever been done before. How could I get to the deepest fibres? How could I totally exhaust my deltoids so they would grow?

Rich Gaspari works at the press behind neck while John Brown spots.

When I was 20 years old I had thought of the solution: Work the shoulders first by tiring them out with an isolation movement and then go to the limit with a general (combination) exercise such as the press behind neck. In order to keep up with the fresh triceps muscles, the already tired deltoid cap would have to really dig down deep to get the power to hoist the resistance. Deeper muscle fibres would be brought into play.

That night I tried out my theory and I could actually feel the deltoids suffering from the unusual practice of following a lighter shoulder isolation exercise with a combination movement. The next day my shoulders were sore to the bone. I was ecstatic!

Pre-exhaustion had arrived! No one seemed to get too excited, but pretty soon Arthur Jones, originator of the famous Nautilus machines, was promoting the principle.

Others to use the pre-exhaustion technique successfully were Mr. America Steve Michalik, and more recently, Mike Mentzer and his brother Ray. Both men have made quite remarkable progress with the principle. Boyer Coe, Scott Wilson, Rachel McLish, and dozens of other champions use the method regularly.

So what is the pre-exhaust system? It is the battering of a specific muscle with a carefully chosen isolation exercise immediately followed by a combination movement. Let's use the pecs as an example. As you may know, the triceps are the weak links involved in many chest exercises. In other words, when you do dips, bench presses, or incline presses, the triceps are worked hard and the pectorals only moderately. This means that your triceps will grow more rapidly than your chest. That's fine if you already have a big chest, but if you want to develop those pecs, then nothing will do it quite as fast as the pre-exhaust method.

The way to get around the "weak-link" triceps is to isolate the pecs first with an exercise like cable crossovers or dumbbell flyes, where the triceps are not directly involved. After a hard set, performing the exercises to the point of failure, proceed *immediately* to the second combination exercise, such as incline presses or bench presses. At the time of doing the presses, the triceps will be *temporarily* stronger than the pectorals, which will be in a state of near exhaustion from the first isolation exercise.

The following exercises can be used for pre-exhaust training:

Thighs
Isolation Movements
Leg Extension, Roman Chair Squats
Combination Movements
Squat, Front Squat, Hack Slide

Thigh Biceps
Isolation Movements
Lying Leg Curl (machine), Standing Leg Curl
Combination Movement
Upside-down Squat (with gravity boots)

Chest
Isolation Movements
Flat Bench Flye, Pulley Crossover, Pec-Deck Flye
Combination Movements
Supine Bench Press, Dumbbell Bench Press

Upper Chest
Isolation Movement
Incline Flye
Combination Movements
Incline Bench Press, Incline Dumbbell Press

Lower Chest
Isolation Movements
Decline Flye, Decline Cable Crossover
Combination Movements
Wide-grip Parallel Bar Dip, Decline Bench Press, Decline Dumbbell Bench Press

Trapezius
Isolation Movements
Shrugs (dumbbells, barbell, calf machine, or bench)
Combination Movements
Upright Row, Smith Machine Clean

Biceps
Isolation Movement
Preacher Bench Curl (dumbbell or barbell)
Combination Movement
Close-undergrip Chin

Triceps
Isolation Movements
Pulley Pressdown, Standing Barbell Extension
Combination Movements
Narrow-grip Bench Press, Parallel Bar Dip

Bev Francis is spotted in her barbell squats by husband Steve Weinberger.

Forearms
Isolation Movement
Reverse Wrist Curl
Combination Movement
Reverse Curl

Rear Shoulders
Isolation Movements
Bent-over Flye, Bent-over Cable Flye, Pec-Deck (reverse position)
Combination Movements
Bent-over Barbell Row, Seated Cable Row

Side Shoulders
Isolation Movements
Lateral Raise, Cable Side Raise
Combination Movements
Upright Row (wide grip), Press behind Neck

Waist
Isolation Movement
Crunch
Combination Movements
Hanging Leg Raise, Inverted Sit-up (with gravity boots)

Back
Isolation Movements
Nautilus Pullover, Barbell Pullover, Parallel Bar Shrugs
Combination Movements
Bent-over Row, Chin to Chest, T-bar Row

Calves
Isolation Movements
Toe Raise (leg-press machine), Standing Calf Raise, Donkey Calf Raise
Combination Movements
Rope Jumping, High Rebounder Jump

1

2

Nautilus pullovers performed by Scott Wilson at Gold's Gym, San Jose.

3

4

Training Frequency

There are definite guidelines here. For the most part, working each muscle group twice a week is ideal in order to work it hard yet also give it recovery time. Some people can add mass by training each muscle group three times a week, but this can lead to overtraining. Of course, if one has a home gym, or goes to a commercial gym that is open every day of the week including holidays, then one does not have to be restricted by the seven-day, man-concocted cycle we humans have chosen to call a week! Here are some time-honored training frequency systems that have proven effective.

Every-Other-Day Split

Mike Mentzer popularized this method, and to this day thousands of bodybuilders find it a very satisfactory way to train. You can build size and mass with this method and you will find that overtraining is almost impossible.

Split your workout into two parts. One of the easiest ways to divide your program is to save all upper body exercises for one training session and all lower body (legs) movements for another. Alternatively, some bodybuilders prefer to do all pulling movements (rowing, curling, chins, wrist curls, etc.) one day and all pushing movements (presses, triceps, stretches, squats) another day. This system is one in which you perform half your workout one day,

Gary Strydom does pulldowns on the lat machine.

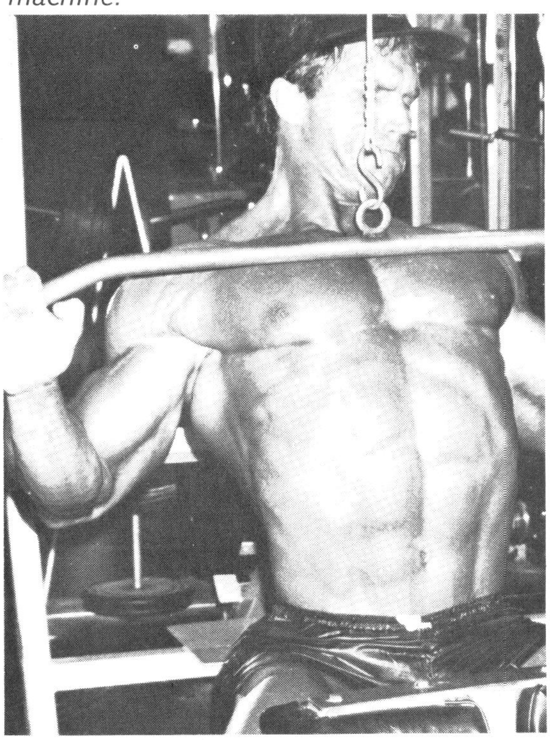

Gary Strydom at start of the lateral raise.

1

2

Jon Jon Park does the hanging leg raise.

3

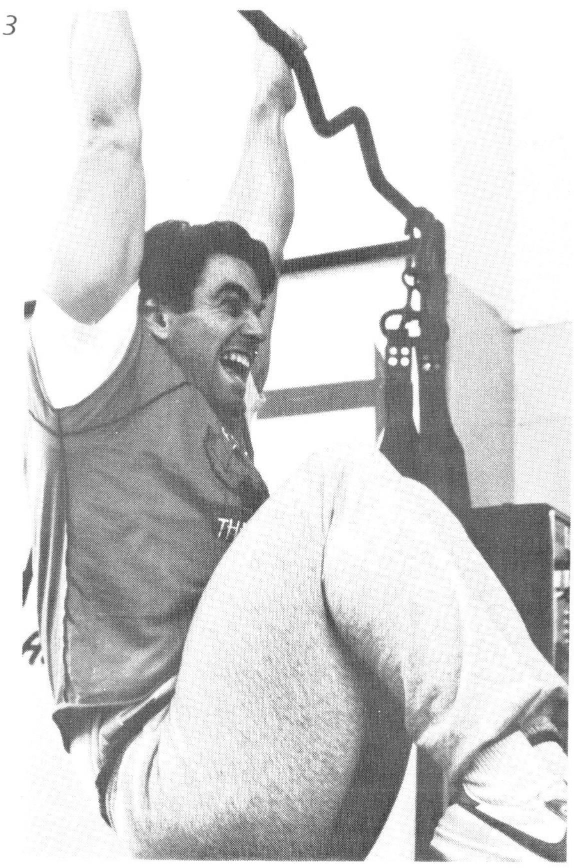

followed by a complete rest the next day. The following day you train the other half of your body and rest again the next day. As you can see, this system does not fit into the conventional seven-day cycle. It is strictly for home trainers or for those who are members of commercial gymnasiums that are open every day of the week.

The great advantage of the every-other-day split method is that once it is underway you never have problems with recuperation. It invariably works out that you are fully recovered and raring to go when your next workout is due. A word of warning: Your rest between workouts is *one* day. Do not ever rest for two days straight. If this happens, you should make up the missed workout by training two days in a row. It is not a good idea to make this a habit.

1

2

Brian Homka works his posterior deltoids as Scott Wilson spots.

3

Canada's Sandra Blackie works on the close-grip chin to chest.

Monday-Wednesday-Friday Routine

This system was used almost exclusively until the 1960s, and even today it is the most popular method of training. You get a full day's rest after each workout, work the entire body three times a week, and have the weekends free for your friends and family. How does it work? You train your whole body in one workout three times a week, allowing at least one day's rest between training sessions on Mondays, Wednesdays and Fridays. But, you may also train Tuesdays, Thursdays and Saturdays, or you can choose Wednesdays, Fridays, and Sundays, etc. The drawback of this system is that you may not be able to do justice to your individual muscles when you have to cram an entire body workout into one training session.

Four-Day Split

This is an off season method of training and is considered a good mass builder for men and women. In the four-day split you train on a seven-day cycle (the traditional week). Split your workout into two parts. Having divided the workout into two equal parts, you perform the first part on Monday, the second part on Tuesday. Wednesday is a rest day. You repeat the first half of the routine on Thursday, and on Friday you do the second half again. The weekends are left free. Your body is completely exercised twice weekly, which is enough to make most people develop.

Six-Day Split

Because you are training each body part three times a week, this method is more severe and can lead to overtraining. It is a favorite system of body-

Brian Homka: bent over T-bar rows. 1 2

John Hnatyschak works on triceps pressdowns.

builders training for an impending contest. Split your workout into two roughly equal parts. Train the first part on Monday, the second part on Tuesday, the first part again on Wednesday, the second part again on Thursday, the first part again on Friday, and the second part again on the Saturday. Sunday is your day off.

Three-Day Split

This method has evolved recently as the most popular system among serious contest trainers, though that is not to say that it can't be used by any and all trainers. A routine doesn't have to be divided into just two parts. There can be value in dividing it into *three*. For example, you could train shoulders and chest one day, legs and back the next day, and biceps, triceps, and waist the third. It would take six consecutive workouts, resting on the seventh day, to accomplish two workouts a week for each body part. The advantage, of course, is that when you only train one or two body parts per workout you can hammer those parts both hard and long. More sets and exercises for those muscle areas can be performed. If you can take it, the three-way split, six-day workout, is ideal for advanced men and women who want to hit their muscles hard with at least three, four, or even five exercises for each part. But it's hard work. Kal Szkalak and Carolyn Cheshire have both used this method extensively.

Britain's Frank Richards.

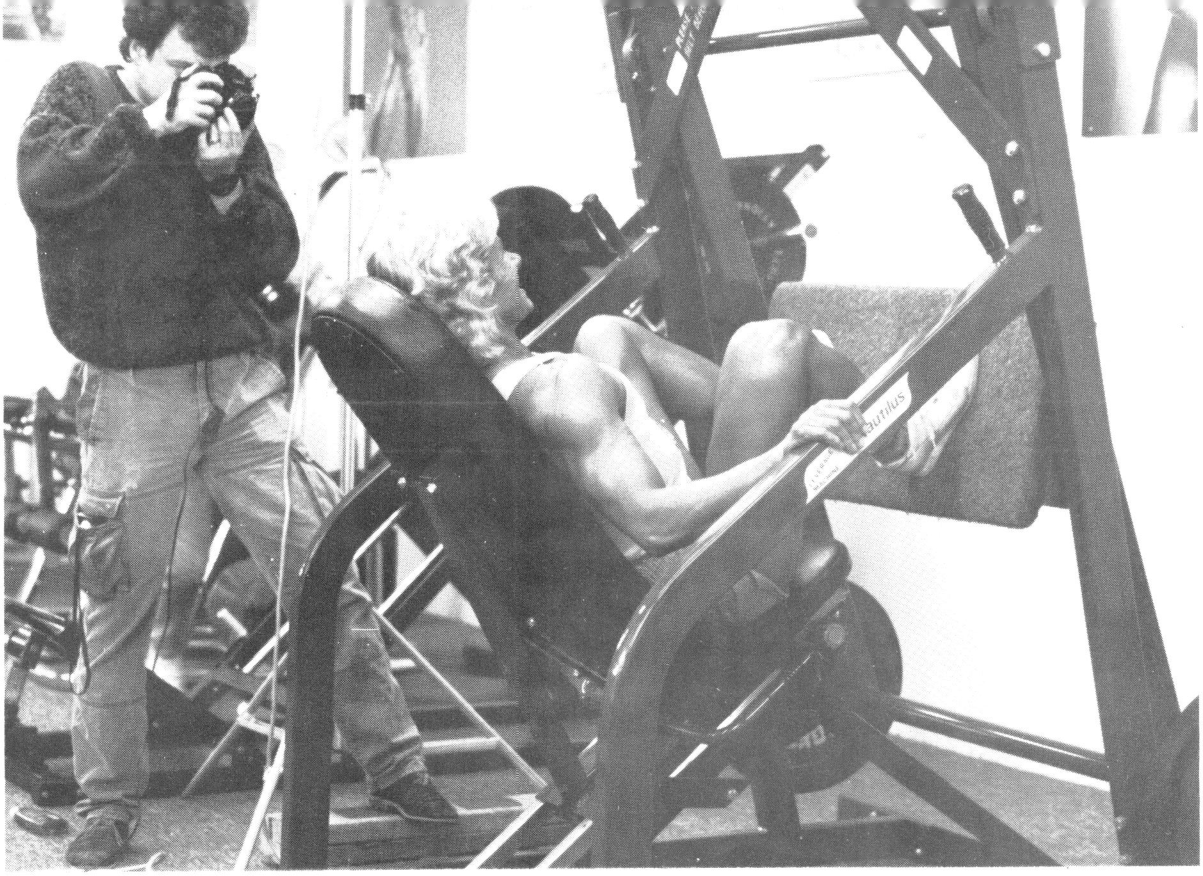

1

2

3

Bev Francis at maximum intensity during a leg press.

4

Thigh extensions by Tony Pearson.

Training Pace

How long you rest between exercises is important to your progress. It is generally accepted that those training for strength, such as power lifters, rest from 3–8 minutes between sets. Bodybuilders are encouraged to rest only one or two minutes between sets. To an extent the rest taken is dictated by the type of exercise you do. Most of us would find no problem in doing a set of curls every 60 seconds, but squatters, for example, would hardly manage to back out of the squat racks in that time, let alone loosen their belts or unbandage their knees.

If you are new to training or just returning after a layoff, then rest until your breath has nearly returned to normal. As you get more fit the rest periods between sets can be gradually shortened. Those wishing to rip up their physiques can create a cardiovascular fat-burning effect by decreasing the time given over to resting between sets of exercise.

It is highly recommended that you take a good rest (15–20 minutes if possible) between working the different body parts. Obviously, this is not practical when training the entire body in one workout, but it is possible when using the popular three-day split routine.

Adding Intensity

To improve in the world of bodybuilding one must add resistance to a level where the muscles are stressed extensively during the final reps of a particular set. The actual poundage used is not the only factor in stressing a muscle, but using a significant weight in each exercise will go a long way towards helping your goal of exhausting the muscle fibres being worked so that they will rebuild tougher. Note Vince Gironda's law: "Train each set as though it were your last. Destroy the muscle; then and only then, move on to the next area."

One can also use *isotension*, the habit of tensing and squeezing a muscle during the exercise performance, particularly at the conclusion of each repetition. This helps break down additional muscle fibres and is made all the more effective by concentrating on making the muscle *feel* the exercise, instead of your thinking about raising up or lifting the resistance. That way you can fatigue the muscle in a quicker and more effective manner and you will develop more mass with this form of training.

1

The upright row demonstrated by Steve Bohnstedt. 3

2

The Mind Pump

A study of the super-ripped upper torso of Serge Nubret.

Lee Haney claims his 4th Olympia title.

Mind pump is my term for keeping mentally strong. Positive thoughts lead to positive aspirations and eventual achievement.

Our minds are like computers. Not only can we switch them on or off as we wish, but we can also switch our thoughts and concentrate on particular problems. The active art of "thinking" is often regarded as hard work, yet once the habit of thinking about problems is acquired, the process becomes almost automatic. Like the computer, our brains can be programmed. We can set goals, motivate ourselves, visualize our success. Ask anyone who has enjoyed a new level of achievement about how they managed to obtain their success. More often than not they will go back in time to a period when they were at an all-time low, and decided that something *must* be done. They made a new mind-set!

Once you have decided what you want, then make your plan of attack. Allocate your time, fuel the fire of hunger for success, and carry out your plan to the letter.

Multi-Ms. Olympia winner Cory Everson and Ben Weider, President of the IFBB.

Motivation

Hooked on bodybuilding? Then you will have no need to drum up more motivation. You will have enough to last a lifetime. Motivation is what drives you forward. You could, however, become a victim of uncontrollable enthusiasm. When this happens, and it's more common than many think, you tend to overwork by training both too long and too frequently. You end up disillusioned and ultimately may give up in disgust.

But for most of us it's time to rekindle the fires of enthusiasm. We need constant inspiration to keep our workouts tough and intense, and to keep on a training diet. If you are currently depressed or in the "workout doldrums," then make up your mind to re-motivate yourself. Take time out to assert your wishes. You *need* success. You *want* to have the best body possible. Don't allow yourself to be self-satisfied. Do not be content with developing a body so that it's just slightly above average. Lack of drive is death. Apathy is your enemy!

If your enthusiasm is lagging, then drum it up by subscribing to the various bodybuilding magazines. Buy hardcore bodybuilding videos. Read all the best books. If you are a home trainer, buy a month's membership at a good heavy-duty gym; the change will work wonders.

Goal Setting

You've heard the one about the uncharted ship. It flopped about in the sea getting nowhere. Why? Because it's course had not been set. Plan where you want to go and how you are going to get there. What do you want out of bodybuilding? Write it down. Set your goal and proceed with confidence.

Remember that anyone can set down a goal of winning the Olympia contest a dozen times. This is sheer foolishness or naivété on their part. Your goals have to be realistic. Set a goal that you can achieve in a two- to three-month time-span. When you reach your target, set a new goal. This is the way to success. Of course you may have secret aspirations of being the world's best body-

Canada's popular Negrita Jayde looks hard as a rock.

It takes effort like this . . .

. . . to get results like this: Shawn Ray, Mr. America.

Dick Baldwin

builder, but keep them in the back of your mind, as a hopeful, but vague possibility. If your small goals are being realized regularly you can then allow this secret long-term aspiration to surface. Ultimately it may be your next realistic step which will put you at the pinnacle of success. It's a good idea to write down your goals. Post them on your notice board where you can see them every day. That will continually remind you of what you are training for. Reinforcing your goals on a regular basis will help steer your actions. Remember you can only achieve what you have first imagined yourself achieving.

Visualization

Arnold Schwarzenegger was one of the first bodybuilders to talk openly about visualization. He said: "When I trained my biceps, I pictured huge mountains, much bigger than biceps can ever be. I knew of course that my biceps are not mountains, but when you positively exaggerate certain things, something happens to your muscles. They react by getting bigger as a result of this strong visualization."

Take weightlifters. They stand in front of a loaded bar before they attempt to lift it. Sometimes they close their eyes to help their concentration. What are they doing? They are visualizing the lift. They "see" themselves lifting the weight before they make the attempt. If they can "see" themselves making the lift, then when it comes to the physical attempt it will be completed without a hitch. But should the lifter have even one percent of doubt in his mind, the lift is lost. Fail mentally and you will fail physically.

Bodybuilders can definitely use vi-

The strongest woman in the world, Bev Francis.

sualization to help them grow. Look at the pictures in this book. Use those images to not only prime your enthusiasm but to also drum up a pump while you're training—that's the mind pump!

After thirty-five years of regular training, attending shows, and interviewing the world's top bodybuilders, I am utterly convinced that with the proper mind-set, we can all achieve far more than we have to date. Use that mind control mechanism attached to your brain. Positively dictate your motivation, your goals and your visualization. See yourself as you want to be, a winner in the world of bodybuilding! Now all you have to do is follow through with the correct physical actions.

Bob Jodkiewicz

Workout Recovery

All the weight training intensity in the world won't help build your body if your system is unable to recuperate fully by the time your next workout rolls around. Recuperation is especially important when we are trying to rip up the physique, because to some extent we are hindering our natural recuperative abilities by:

- Increasing training frequency.
- Consuming less food.
- Adding extra resistance exercises.
- Performing additional sets and reps.

It is therefore important that when we decrease calories to cut-up, we must also make certain that the food we eat is 100 percent nutritious, and that junk foods that are fattening but nutritionally empty are eliminated from the diet. High on your list of foods to help fully recover from your workouts should be animal proteins and citrus fruits.

As far as exercise is concerned, there are a few pointers that will help recovery. Do not suddenly involve yourself with numerous sets of *new* exercises. Always introduce a new exercise (or an exercise that you haven't performed for some months or years) slowly. One or two sets is sufficient to begin with. If you start a new movement with five or six heavy sets you run the risk of throwing off your recovery ability. The same can occur if you perform too many sets of a single exercise, or if you use too much intensity (such as with forced reps) for too long a period.

Diana Dennis outside Gold's Gym in Venice, California.

Steve Bohnstedt (center) poses with L.A. Raiders Jeff Barnes and Lyndon King.

We have to train the body without fatiguing it beyond its power of swift efficient recovery. If we cannot heal and rebuild muscle tissue between workouts we are overtraining. If unchecked, this will eventually lead to flat-looking muscles, loss of tone and a reduction in muscle mass. You might also suffer persistent soreness and stiffness in the muscles and joints, nervousness, depression, headaches, diarrhea, sluggishness or loss of appetite.

What speeds recuperation? Probably the first aspect that comes to mind is rest and relaxation. After all, it is when we are at rest or asleep that our muscles recover from the workout. We all have different ways to relax. With some it is listening to music. Others like to enjoy art, poetry, conversation, writing, videos, religion, books, or television. I suspect most bodybuilders prefer to relax with their favorite muscle mag. The important thing is to put your feet up and relax.

Stress management is another important aspect that we must pay attention to if we are going to recover quickly from our training. Sometimes over-enthusiasm can drain us physically and mentally. Some of us want bodybuilding success so badly that we just *can't wait* for it to happen. We get over-anxious and over-stressed. This results in poor recuperation. Try to control your emotions. Think carefully before acting on important issues involving money, love, friendships, schoolwork, study, or business. Chronically recurring stress drains the body of energy and interferes with our ability to recuperate and improve our physical appearance.

Always try to get plenty of fresh air and sunshine. Both aid recovery from strenuous workouts. If you work in a windowless environment, then getting out into natural light is imperative. Fresh air, deeply breathed, energizes the body. In fact, many believe that an athlete's total success depends on the amount of oxygen he can consume. Didn't Arnold Schwarzenegger and Franco Columbu make the best gains of their lives when training at Gold's Gym in Venice, while inhaling pure oxygen from divers' oxygen tanks between heavy sets of exercise?

Are not bodybuilders who train in warm, sunny climes usually more successful than those who have to live and train among stuffy, centrally heated surroundings or in dark basement gyms?

Strongly yours: Steve Weinberger kisses wife and gym partner Bev Francis.

You may marvel at the way some bodybuilders manage to train. They hit the weights hard, day after day, and still recuperate and grow steadily. It should be noted here and now that most top-rated bodybuilders take steroids, a practice definitely not recommended. Many

Clare Furr and Trent Mitchell.

Jusup Wilcosz and his wife.

Don Ross, Samantha Madsen, and Tommy Lamparski show off their gains.

serious bodybuilders have become very sick as a result of taking steroids without a proper doctor's prescription and the attendant monitoring of their vital functions. Why do I mention steroids? Because they artificially aid recovery from bodybuilding workouts, abnormally so. I wouldn't want you to think that you were in some way deficient by comparing your recovery ability to a steroid-taking bodybuilder. Have I taken steroids? No. Have I been tempted? Yes. Why didn't I try steroids? Outright fear! Of course, I do have an insight into the subject that few in the sport can equal. As publisher of *MuscleMag International*, I am the steady recipient of mail from readers who have suffered terrible experiences with these muscle-growth drugs. I have a file with over one hundred letters marked "steroid horror stories." Besides, steroids end up misshaping the body. The shoulders bunch up, the waist gets enormous, the face becomes lined and invariably widens (the gaps between the teeth widen too). Men can develop gynecomastia (breast overdevelopment) and women may develop excessive facial hair. Now do you still wonder why I'm not in favor of steroids?

Aerobics

Rich Gaspari in winning form.

Before you turn to the chapter on the diet regimen you will be following, this chapter will show how aerobic exercise is another way to lower your body-fat percentage besides just eating fewer calories. Exercise affects the basal metabolic rate (BMR), and the BMR affects how efficiently fat is used or stored. The goal is to increase your metabolic rate in order to burn calories at a faster rate. Doing aerobic exercise is easier than turning down that dish of ice cream!

Adjusting Your Metabolism

What is the metabolic rate? It is the rate at which our body burns up energy, the speed of our various body processes.

We all know people, invariably super-thin, who are highly strung, who walk fast, talk fast and seem to be forever on the go. This typifies the individual with a fast metabolism. Gaining weight for these people is a problem. They are usually so hyped-up that almost everything they eat is burned up in an ever-roaring energy furnace.

At the other extreme, the slow metabolism is depicted by the slow-moving, slow-talking individual who is overweight and lethargic. Oddly, people like this have *thrifty*, or efficient, cells. When they eat, their body only uses a small amount of the food; the remaining calories go to the fat cells for storage.

Aaron Baker

Posing is second nature to Cory Everson.

Actually, extremes in BMR, either high or low, are not conducive to success. If you suspect that you are either the hyper type or the slothful type then you need to act positively to bring your BMR to normal.

Women are sometimes at a slight disadvantage in respect to BMR in comparison to men, but BMR is not genetically determined once and for all. We *can* do something about it, whether we are male or female, short or tall, young or not so young.

After the age of 20 there is a natural and gradual slowing down of the metabolic rate each year. This may be good news for the individual yearning to add weight, but not such great news for the person wanting to rip up. Those who want to rid their body of fat so that their muscles are defined should take steps to increase their metabolic rates so that fat cells are burned up.

How do we increase our metabolic rates to burn calories at a faster rate? How can we burn up more calories even while at rest, rid ourselves of sluggishness, and peel off fat and take on a more muscular appearance? To rev up your metabolism and drop unwanted pounds consider these guidelines:

- Cut calories, but not drastically. Consume plenty of natural foods such as fruits, vegetables, and complex carbohydrates such as grain. Two-thirds of your diet should consist of complex carbohydrates. Keep fat consumption low. If you cut calories too drastically, your body can construe the food reduction as a signal that starvation is at hand. Your BMR will react by slowing down even more to conserve energy reserves.

- Increase training frequency. It may not be a bad idea to train each body part 2½ to 3 times a week for a while. This added activity will serve to keep your tick-over speed revved up. Extra calories will be burned and additional fat will be lost.
- Go for a walk after meals. The inclination is to remain motionless after eating. Sluggishness creeps in. But mild exercise (not heavy workouts or aerobics) will help use up calories before they have a chance to be stored up as fat.
- Avoid simple carbohydrates—candy, desserts, soft drinks, sugar, ice cream, etc.

Alternate dumbbell row performed by Jim Quinn: start.

Alternate dumbbell row: finish.

- Keep the temperature in your home on the low side. When the body is cool, the system is forced to compensate by increasing BMR. Do not take this advice to extremes, however. Wearing too few clothes or keeping the temperature below 65°F would be inviting pneumonia.
- Maintain your progressive resistance exercises. One of the rewards of weight training is that the muscle mass, by its very existence, increases metabolic rate. The more muscle you build, the more fat you burn. More calories are burned by your system at any moment, day or night, because muscle is *active* tissue. The more lean muscle you carry on your frame, the higher your metabolic rate is likely to be.

- Add some aerobic exercise to your curriculum. Each week aim for three separate sessions of up to 30 minutes each. Researchers at the University of New Hampshire have scientifically proven that aerobically active individuals who regularly participate in aerobic activities such as jogging, swimming, rowing, stair climbing, aerobic dance, mountaineering, cross-country skiing, or circuit training, burn increased numbers of calories, even when not exercising.

Once you perk up your metabolism, you will feel more alert and alive, but be warned it could revert back to sluggishness if you take prolonged breaks from your exercise regimen, or if your diet contains too many calories.

Aerobic activity is one way to help the body to rip up.

Aerobics: Fat-to-Muscle Exercise

Aerobic exercise improves the strength of the heart and lungs, thus benefiting circulation. It keeps us super-fit. However, the bodybuilder has a special reason for performing aerobics. When aerobic activity is performed regularly and for the correct length of time and frequency, not only does your body become a better machine, it *looks* like a better machine, because regular aerobic activity burns off fat! Ideally, bodybuilders should always perform some aerobic activity in their training, but this, especially with men, is seldom the case. Aerobics are usually only included during the ripping-up phase. Typically, this is the last two or three months prior to competition. In order to be effective, aerobic activity should be practiced as follows:

- The exercise should be performed for a minimum of two, preferably three or even four days a week on alternate days when possible.
- The exercise should be performed at a suitable level of intensity for 20 to 40 minutes' duration each session.
- Maximum benefit is achieved when an intensity level of 70–80 percent of your maximum heart rate is achieved.

Which Aerobic Sport?

For fitness (as opposed to ripping up), ideal aerobic activities include jogging, aerobic dance, swimming, cycling, brisk walking, rowing, stair climbing, cross-country skiing, rope jumping, the stationary bike, running in place, basketball, handball, squash, skating, racquetball, hill climbing, running the bleachers,

Gary Strydom caught during a set of triceps pressdowns.

Aaron Baker demonstrates alternate dumbbell curls.

etc. However, the pure bodybuilder is concerned with losing a minimal amount of muscle mass while shedding the maximum amount of fat. This fact necessarily eliminates such activities as swimming, basketball, racquetball and cross-country skiing, all of which involve too much high-repetition use of the arms: The high rate of activity will cause the arms to lose too much muscle mass. The proven most effective aerobic movement to help a serious bodybuilder reduce his body fat level is stationary bike riding, although some have found success with regular bike riding, fast walking, and jogging.

Target Heart Rate

Earlier I said that maximum aerobic benefit is achieved when an intensity level of 70–80 percent of your maximum heart rate is achieved. How do you calculate your *maximum heart rate*? The most accepted formula to determine your personal maximum heart rate is

220 − your age = Maximum Heart Rate (MHR).

Warning: This is considered the maximum degree of heart overexertion and is never recommended as a figure to sustain during exercise. As suggested earlier, the best level for exercise (known as your target heart rate zone) is 70–80 percent of your maximum heart rate. The formula needed to ascertain your Target Heart Rate (THR) is:

Maximum Heart Rate × 0.7 = 70 percent intensity

Maximum Heart Rate × 0.8 = 80 percent intensity

You will notice that a sustained program of aerobic activity gives you new pep, a lower fat percentage, and greater fitness than you previously enjoyed. Your *resting* heartbeat will slow down as your heart gains new strength and efficiency.

Gary Strydom keeps an eye on Holland's Juliette Bergman while she performs the triceps extension exercise.

Ulf Larsen of Sweden.

Eating to Get Ripped

Most people have to diet in order to rip up. Those lucky few who do not either have engines that are constantly running at boiling point, or else they spend three to five hours a day performing aerobic exercises. Unless you have the metabolic rate of an attacking lion, I suggest you make use of the nutritional advice in this chapter.

Some people say diet is fifty percent or even seventy percent of getting ripped. Whatever the ratio, we do know that it's extremely important. An ordinary person with 18–30 percent body fat cannot get ripped and cut by using bodybuilding exercises exclusively. Forget barbells and dumbbells for a minute and let's talk *diet change*.

Cutting up that body of yours will require that you eat fewer calories. Simple enough! you say. But there's more to it than that. Not only do we have to eat smaller amounts of food, but we must also make sure that the food we eat is the most nutritious available. Also, getting psyched for your workouts is much easier than staying on a strict diet 24 hours a day. Getting ripped has to be preceded by a conscious and deliberate *mind-set*. You *are* going to succeed. You *will* follow through with the diet requirements. Use the pictures in this book to keep the images of *success* in your mind.

The vascular look is demonstrated by Craig Monson.

Greg Comeau

Diet Fads

Bodybuilding diets have gone through stages. At the beginning of the century the *strongmen* of the day (the term bodybuilder hadn't been coined) would exercise with their barbells and dumbbells, and then in order to "feed" their muscles they would down a few quarts of beer. Brew was actually considered to be the best "food" for increasing pure strength.

The seventies brought us the bulk craze. Milk stood as a substitute for beer. It did a better job of building the body but hardly contributed to fitness or even the appearance of fitness, according to scientific information we have today.

Today, things have changed in order to exploit new discoveries in nutrition. Modern bodybuilders drink less beer, consume low-fat milk, and incredible as it may seem to the old-timers, they actually perform aerobic exercise. This chapter explains the current nutritional strategies.

Arnold Schwarzenegger reigned supreme during the bulk period of bodybuilding.

Calorie Counting Theory

When you take in as many calories as your body burns up you are in thermodynamic balance. Should you ingest fewer calories than you burn up you will lose weight. Eat more and you will gain.

Look at it like a bank account. You start with a given amount of money in the bank (fat on your body). Eating and drinking corresponds to making deposits. Exercise (walking, working out, running) can be regarded as writing a check. If your deposits equal your withdrawals, your balance (weight) will stay the same. Burn more calories than you consume and your body will start losing weight.

It is an accepted opinion that a person leading a moderately active lifestyle needs 15 calories per pound of body weight, every day. If you have a desired weight you want to achieve, then multiply that weight by 15 and the answer is the number of calories you need to ingest daily. For example, if you want to weigh 150 pounds you should be eating 2,250 calories a day just to keep that weight. If you want to weigh 185, then take in 2,775 calories. Two hundred and twenty-five pounds requires a 3,375 calorie daily input, while a 110-pound body weight requires only 1,650.

According to calorie counting theory, if you eliminate just one pat of butter a day, you won't deposit some 3,780 calories each month! This represents about one pound of fat "burned off"—twelve pounds a year. Eliminate two pats of butter a day and you'll lose about half a pound a week, twenty-four pounds a year. As a quick guide you can estimate that a "cut" of 500 calories per day will take off about one pound a week, fifty pounds in a year! A daily cut of 1,000

Gladys Portugues keeps her legs looking great with the help of leg extensions.

Ming Chew of New York shows impressive vascular development.

calories will leave you two pounds lighter every week, and so on. The same arithmetic applies if you want to gain weight.

Now back to real life. Ok, I can hear you. Many of you will be saying that you eat lower calories than I am recommending, yet the results are not apparent. That only goes to prove that the thermodynamic system outlined above is too simplistic. The main obstacle to the thermodynamic system's efficiency is the *metabolism*. Extremely severe diets—those that verge on starvation—frequently cause the metabolism to slow down dramatically (to prepare for what the body thinks is the coming famine). This is what happens to hibernating mammals who go without food all winter. Cut calories too drastically and you may *prevent* significant weight loss. Cutting calories gradually over a period of time is more effective.

Trying to figure out the *exact* calorie intake of every meal is impossible, but know the ballpark calorie content of your food. Without becoming a "numbers fanatic" you should have a pretty fair idea of approximately how many calories you are consuming daily. Check food labels and those inexpensive calorie-counter booklets. Keep close to the calorie level you are shooting for and know which foods, like butter, cream, and salad dressing, are high-calorie foods that you should avoid.

Ripped and ready, Gary Strydom's hardness is difficult to beat.

Fat Reduction

There is another snag besides the metabolism to be considered when we talk about fat reduction. Those of us who were fat babies or who were overfed as infants may be carrying more fat cells than the average person. As a result, this frequently makes the job of ripping up even more difficult. A very few of us have glandular or severe metabolic disorders which lead to obesity, but the rest of us are overweight for one or more of the following reasons: We eat and drink too much, we eat the wrong foods, or we do not exercise enough. For bodybuilders it's likely to be the first two. We've already covered the first reason, so let's take a closer look at what *kind* of foods we should eat.

Calorie reduction is the secret to losing body fat, but there are a few provisos. Don't think that you can eat just any kind of food so long as your calorie target is met. This is often claimed, but it is nonsense. Since you're eating less on a training diet, the food you do eat has to be packed with nutrition. High calorie, fat-loaded and nutritionally empty "junk foods" have no place in your training diet. They will keep you smooth in spite of all your hard work.

I'll be the first to admit that I'm not a health-food fanatic. Few bodybuilders are. Nevertheless, the individual wanting to get ripped to the bone should eliminate the following foods: Candies, cookies, cakes, chocolate bars, white or devitalized bread, table salt, table sugar, puddings, doughnuts, bacon, pizza, hot dogs, smoked or processed meats, potato chips, pretzels, ice cream, pies, beer, liquor, soft drinks, whipped cream, jams, salad dressings, and sugar-loaded breakfast cereals. These foods tend to clog up the system, interfere with energy levels, and contribute to obesity and disease.

Anja Langer stretches her calves before getting into heavy lower leg work.

I can hear you now. Yipes. What *can* we eat? Read on for the recommended foods in the ripping-up diet, complete with menus.

The Ripping-Up Diet

Remember that good nutrition is balanced nutrition. You need to include food from each of the following categories every day, except perhaps during the last weeks prior to an important contest where you have to appear cut-to-ribbons.

Milk (milk, yogurt, cottage cheese, hard cheese)
Meat (beef, veal, lamb, fish, poultry, eggs)
Vegetables (fruits, nuts, vegetables, legumes)
Grains (breads, rice, cereals)
Fats (butter, margarine, oils)

Get the low-fat, diet varieties of the milk group. The last group, fats, should be consumed in very small quantities.

Some of the very best foods we can eat are the following: Fruit, bran, beans, cabbage, carrots, fish, garlic and onions, kale, liver, melons, nuts, oysters, soybeans, seeds, poultry, sweet potatoes, wheat germ, yogurt, whole grain products such as whole grain cereals and whole wheat breads (especially if there's no added sugar or sodium), and natural fresh vegetables (steamed or raw).

Never fry meat, vegetables, potatoes, fish or eggs. Try not to remove edible peels from fruits and vegetables (wash them first, though, since they may have been sprayed with insecticides). Add lemon juice or a little vinegar to a salad rather than bottled dressings. Never add table salt or table sugar to foods—Mother Nature has already provided both naturally in fruits and vegetables. Instead, you may add natural herbs and spices. Since we need fibre, always try to eat an apple rather than apple juice; an orange rather than orange juice. There is a difference.

Protein

Protein is essential to everyone, but is especially important to bodybuilders. It is vital for successful bodybuilding. Without sufficient quantities of protein, no gains will materialize.

British bodybuilding nutritionist Bernard Beverley said: "Of the three major elements in your diet—carbohydrate, fat and protein—protein is the most important because it is the only thing from which your body can recreate cells and stimulate growth. The two other items are primarily needed for energy. Protein is the constructor of the body."

When you exercise, the muscle cells are broken down and it is the ingested protein that enables them to build up during rest. What some bodybuilders fail to realize is that protein is also required for many vital bodily functions, including the production of blood and hormones. Your teeth, bones, and even your hair need protein.

The foods we eat can change our metabolic rates. Curiously, the greatest increase in metabolic activity occurs when we eat high protein foods. In fact the mere act of eating protein raises metabolism 30 percent above our basal metabolic rate (BMR) while fat raises it 4 percent and carbohydrates six percent. In short, the body works harder to metabolize protein than any other food.

If you take in more protein than you need, you'll absorb what you do need much easier. A hard-training bodybuilder would probably require about one gram of protein per pound of body weight to significantly increase muscle mass. Best protein foods include eggs, milk, organ meats (liver is excellent), red meats, poultry, fish, cheese, and nuts.

A bodybuilder should always eat carbohydrates whenever he eats protein. If you do not have complex carbohydrates (vegetables, breads, cereals, rice, and fruit) present with your protein, your system will convert the protein, not into amino acids as it should to build muscle, but into urea, which is eliminated in your urine. You may not need huge amounts of complex carbohydrates, but some are required each time you ingest a protein food.

Getting Started on the Ripping Up Diet

The dietary secret of losing fat is to eat fresh wholesome foods from each of the five major food groups, but to consume fewer calories per day than your body needs for weight maintenance. When you go on a calorie-reduced diet, it is important that you do not drastically reduce your food intake at any one time. You must cut calories slowly. For example, when you first start on a diet, simply exchange an apple for your dessert, or eliminate all butter from your diet. The next week you can cut down slightly on your meat and potato portions. This *gradual* tightening up of the diet is ideal because drastic cuts cause hunger pangs, headaches and even sickness. The body often interprets huge calorie cuts as a period of oncoming starvation and fat deposits are actually preserved.

Eat a wholesome breakfast. It will set you up correctly for the day and should be the most nutritious (and biggest) meal of the day. You know the saying: "Eat breakfast like a king, lunch like a prince and dinner like a pauper."

If the weight is coming off too fast and you are losing muscle mass instead of fat, then eat a few more calories and especially keep your protein intake moderately high. Should the opposite be true, and you are not noticing any definition, then cut down on your calorie intake even more.

Massive bodybuilder Jim Quinn.

Bodybuilders with unwanted padding at stomach and hips often find that after a week or two of dieting they may actually look worse than they did before starting the diet. This is normal. When initial fat deposits are burned up, the skin loosens somewhat. Not to worry. Keep to your program and your body-fat percentage level will be reduced enough to show your rock-hard, shapely muscles.

The following are some daily examples of good nutrition at different calorie levels. You will have to tailor the actual calorie amounts of each day according to your own calorie requirements for weight gain, loss, or maintenance.

Breakfast Suggestions

	Calories
½ cup oatmeal	65
½ banana	50
½ cup 2% milk	62
coffee/tea	
Total calories	**177**

	Calories
1 poached egg on whole wheat toast	152
½ grapefruit sweetened with artificial sweetener	50
coffee/tea	
Total calories	**202**

	Calories
½ cup orange juice	55
½ cup cottage cheese (lowfat, low sodium)	85
½ tomato, sliced	18
1 slice whole wheat toast with 1 tsp. margarine	105
coffee/tea	
Total calories	**263**

	Calories
½ cup oatmeal	65
1 cup skim milk	90
½ cup fresh fruit salad (artificially sweetened)	70
1 slice of whole wheat toast with 1 tsp. margarine	105
coffee/tea	
Total calories	**330**

	Calories
½ cup strawberries	27
2 boiled eggs	160
1 slice whole wheat toast	72
1 tsp. margarine	33
½ cup skim milk	45
coffee/tea	
Total calories	**337**

	Calories
1 fresh orange	65
1 cheese omelette made with 2 egg whites, 1 yolk, 1 tsp. grated cheddar (cooked in Pam)	125
1 slice back (lean) bacon	65
2 slices whole wheat toast	144
Total calories	**399**

	Calories
1 salmon omelette made with 2 egg whites, 1 yolk, 1½ oz. salmon (cooked in Pam)	155
2 slices whole wheat toast with 1 tsp. margarine	175
½ cup sliced peaches	32
½ cup 2% milk	62
Total calories	**424**

	Calories
½ cup grapefruit juice	47
2 shredded wheat biscuits	160
1 cup 2% milk	123
1 boiled egg	80
1 slice whole wheat toast	72
Total calories	**482**

Snack Suggestions

	Calories
carrot stick	10
celery stick	10
½ cup cottage cheese (lowfat, low sodium)	85
Total calories	**105**
6 oz. yogurt (partly skimmed, unflavored)	112
½ cup strawberries	27
Total calories	**139**
1 cup skim milk	90
1 bran muffin	85
Total calories	**175**
5 dried apricots	100
½ cup yogurt	80
Total calories	**180**
1 apple	70
1″ cube of cheddar cheese	116
Total calories	**186**
1 strawberry protein shake made with 1 cup 2% milk, 2 tbsp. milk and egg protein, sweetened with 1 tbsp. honey, ½ cup strawberries	
Total calories	**240**
1 banana shake made with 1 banana, 1 tbsp. honey, 2 tbsp. milk and egg protein, and 1 cup 2% milk	
Total calories	**250**

Gary Strydom

Lunch Suggestions

	Calories
mineral water	
3 oz. slice chicken	150
4 slices melba toast	60
1 strip each of green and red pepper, celery and carrot	30
Total calories	**240**

	Calories
½ cup cottage cheese (lowfat, low sodium)	85
assorted fresh fruit (½ apple sliced, ½ peach sliced, ½ cup grapes, sliced melon)	112
4 slices melba toast	60
tea/coffee	
Total calories	**257**

	Calories
3 oz. broiled halibut	130
1 cup brussels sprouts	55
baked potato	90
½ cup sliced fresh pineapple (unsweetened)	38
tea/coffee	
Total calories	**313**

	Calories
1 cup 2% milk	123
Open-face salmon sandwich (made with 3 oz. salmon, chopped celery, 1 tsp. yogurt) on one slice whole wheat toast	210
tossed salad with lemon juice	60
Total calories	**393**

	Calories
mixed salad (tomato, lettuce, cucumber, green pepper chunks topped with 1 oz. shredded cheddar cheese)	281
1 slice whole wheat pita bread	72
1 apple	70
Total calories	**423**

	Calories
1 cup tomato juice (low sodium)	45
tuna salad sandwich (3 oz. tuna, 1 tsp. plain yogurt, chopped celery, ½ tsp. dill), 2 slices whole wheat bread, lettuce	325
carrot sticks	20
½ cup fresh fruit salad (unsweetened)	65
Total calories	**455**

	Calories
sliced turkey sandwich on whole wheat bread, 3 oz. turkey, sliced tomato, lettuce	334
½ cup fresh fruit salad (unsweetened)	65
1 cup skim milk	90
Total calories	**489**

	Calories
1 cup 2% milk	123
cheddar and tomato sandwich on rye bread (1 oz. cheddar)	312
mixed salad with vinegar or lemon juice	60
1 banana	100
Total calories	**595**

Dinner Suggestions

	Calories
3 oz. broiled unskinned chicken breast	115
½ cup steamed green beans	15
½ cup steamed carrots	20
⅓ cup brown rice	65
½ cup fresh fruit salad (artificially sweetened)	60
Total calories	**275**

	Calories
cucumber salad (1 cup sliced cucumber with 2 tbsp. plain yogurt, 1 tsp. vinegar and ½ pkg. artificial sweetener)	20
broiled sole (3 oz.)	172
boiled rice (⅓ cup)	65
½ cup steamed carrots	20
½ cup sliced strawberries and bananas	50
Total calories	**327**

	Calories
Spanish omelette (2 eggs, sliced tomatoes, green pepper chunks, mushrooms, cooked in Pam)	215
1 slice whole wheat toast	80
½ cup spinach	20
½ cup raspberries, artificially sweetened	35
Total calories	**350**

	Calories
½ cup tomato juice	22
2 slices broiled calves' liver	147
½ cup steamed cabbage sprinkled with caraway seeds	18
baked potato	90
baked apple	90
Total calories	**367**

	Calories
3 oz. lean broiled veal chop	150
½ cup steamed green beans	15
½ cup steamed mushrooms	10
1 broiled tomato	35
½ cup noodles sprinkled with 1 tbsp. Parmesan cheese	100
1 apple	90
Total calories	**400**

	Calories
3 oz. lean ground beef patty, broiled	185
½ cup steamed broccoli	45
sliced tomatoes and cucumbers	45
baked potato	90
1 banana	100
Total calories	**465**

	Calories
broiled shish-kebab (made with 3 oz. lean beef)	165
1 slice whole wheat pita bread	140
tossed salad with 1 tbsp. low calorie dressing	90
1 apple	70
Total calories	**465**

	Calories
(3 oz.) broiled steak	330
baked potato	90
tossed salad	65
½ cup cantaloupe stuffed with strawberries (artificially sweetened)	80
Total calories	**565**

Dorothy Herndon

Supplements

Supplements of one kind or another are becoming more and more important to bodybuilders who want to develop rock-hard bodies. Traditional aids include kelp as an iodine source, protein powder for muscle bulk, Vitamin C for tissue repair, Vitamin B_3 (niacin) as a vasodilator during contests, choline and inositol (components of Vitamin B_8) as fat-emulsifiers, and the newer free-form amino acids (the building blocks of protein) for hardness, mass and cuts.

Today, more and more substances are coming onto the market (sometimes the black market) which are actual drugs. They may be prescription drugs, but there are plenty of sports medicine doctors who are little more than drug dispensers or "gym pushers." They want your money more than they care about your well-being. They will prescribe dangerous steroid or hormone drugs that can damage the most healthy of bodies. I have personally witnessed steroid abuse, especially among enthusiastic young bodybuilders who wanted instant fame. Many damaged themselves permanently in their quest for bodybuilding fame. Do not be one of them!

Some substances such as vitamins and minerals can make you mildly sick if taken in the wrong quantities. Some are drugs intended for completely different purposes than bodybuilding, such as Novaldex, an estrogen antagonist meant to combat breast cancer tumors in

John Hnatyschak

women, but used by bodybuilders to eliminate water retention; and human growth hormone (HGH) taken from cadavers (dead bodies) and originally used in the treatment of dwarfism, but used by bodybuilders to rip up. It increases the likelihood of diabetes and heart attack in later years. Thyroxin, also used for ripping up, stimulates the thyroid gland but when used too long can shut down the thyroid gland completely, creating a lifelong dependency on the drug.

Why do bodybuilders take these substances when there are so many harmful side effects associated with them? Because they think the bad stuff will happen to the other guy, and because they're so shortsighted they can't see beyond the next contest. Mainly they do it because they want to win, and they think that these substances are requirements for winning. Some people think that drugs are a magic shortcut to a winning physique. Take lasix, for example. It's a strong diuretic often referred to as "the last chance drug," used by bodybuilders who cannot or will not diet strictly. It works, but can cause cramps, faintness, and a flat appearance.

People want magic pills—but remember that even steroids do nothing if you don't train. These things won't make you win if you haven't done the basic training and dieting—and even then they only give a *slight* edge and cannot guarantee you so much as a tenth place trophy!

Competition:

Whatever you wear, you can't hide real muscles: Ed Kawak, Berry DeMey, Bertil Fox, and Albert Beckles.

The Winning Attitude

When you choose to enter bodybuilding competition you are almost certainly headed for severe disappointment unless you are competing for the enjoyment of self improvement as well as to win. There is enjoyment and satisfaction in climbing the competitive ladder when you are beginning your bodybuilding career, but not if you take winning too seriously.

I have seen men and women on their way up ecstatic with happiness at placing in the top six at a state level show. On the other hand, I can't count the times when I have observed the second place person in a Mr. or Ms. Olympia become *totally* devastated at failing to win. Let's face it, everyone who becomes eligible for an Olympia competition is a winner; yet I have seen place winners feeling so low in self worth after failing to win that they looked like they were ready to jump off a skyscraper. They felt like real losers when the opposite was obviously true.

You must bodybuild for yourself. Strive to reach your full potential and you will be a winner. Judge yourself by your own progress. When you are a bodybuilder, whether you are stripped for the beach, wearing a T-shirt and jeans, or fully dressed in a three-piece suit, people will notice that you are *built*. You feel special. But if you invest emotionally in only settling for the top you are doomed to disappointment and heartache. Do not set unrealistic goals.

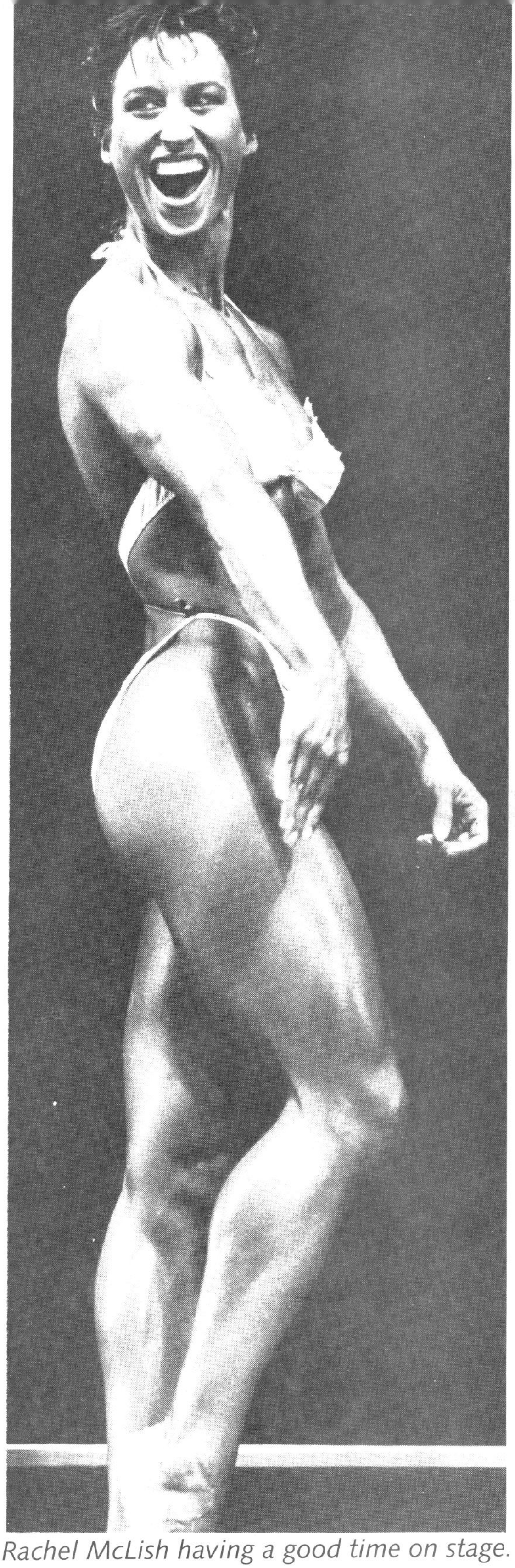

Rachel McLish having a good time on stage.

Brian Buchannan and Mike Christian.

Be realistic about being *the greatest*. Only one person can win the big "O" every year, and it's likely that such a person will be a genetic superior. Things are certainly different from the early Mr. and Ms. Olympia contests. Back then clever trainers with something less than a perfect wide shouldered, narrow hipped, fully muscular body could and did win. But those days are gone forever.

Shed your tears now and then get back to training. Build the strongest, sexiest, most ripped body on *your* beach. Wanna enter contests? Go ahead, but don't let defeat blow your mind. You can do everything humanly known to get ready for a show and still not take home a first place trophy. If success or near success on the posing platform comes your way then savor it and press onward. But don't place your mental well-being on the line by putting everything into beating Arnold Schwarzenegger's 7-time Olympia winning streak, especially if you haven't yet even won a local title.

Have you noticed that many bodybuilders also become successful in other endeavors? It's true. Any experienced bodybuilder knows that the benefits of weight training extend to life in general. Confidence, poise and self image are apparent in any bodybuilder. The disciplines that you need to become a great athlete can also be applied to excelling in other adventures, to succeeding in life itself.

So, become a good bodybuilder and watch the rest of your life fall into place. Your commitment to looking good will spill over to make you a success in any other achievement to which you set your mind.

Mike Christian, Alan Dalfen, and Pete Grymkowski.

Countdown to Competition

Ron Love, Michael Ashley, and Shane Dimora

For the person who wants to go the distance, getting into contest condition is the ultimate goal. At contest time bodybuilders, both men and women, have to be cut to the bone. It requires a serious attitude. You need to underscore your efforts with savage determination. Yes, you can do it, but you will be going beyond the realms of ripped. You will be pushing back the boundaries of super-muscularity known in the annals of bodybuilding as being positively . . . shredded!

Getting your body fat level down to a lean 8–12 percent or less is the most important thing you can do so that your muscles, shaped by hard training, are shown to maximum effect at contest time. Your body takes on a completely new appearance where veins and even cross-striations of the muscles can be seen as clearly as on an anatomy chart.

This shredded condition that is sought after by so many and achieved by so few is so severe that the athlete only maintains this degree of combined "separation, mass, and definition" for a few days at most, and sometimes for only as little as a few hours. It could be considered an unhealthy condition since body fat levels are extremely low. After the contest, win or lose, most bodybuilders dive for the ice cream in an effort to appease their yearning for fat, sugar, and milk, three ingredients they have gone without during their days and weeks of arduous contest preparation.

Negrita Jayde concentrates on triceps pressdowns.

Heavyweight world champ: Luiz Freitas of Brazil.

3 Months and Counting: Diet

Probably the greatest mistake made when it comes to contest preparation is that the bodybuilder starts dieting *too late*. If you still have to lose weight right up to the competition, you've lost the contest. You should have started your diet earlier. It is far better to sensibly diet for three months prior to a show than to cram the process into a single month or less, all but starving yourself in the process. People who do this invariably find that instead of ending up with a tight, muscular physique, they display a flat body, often with loose skin around the midsection and lower back from abrupt weight loss. Bear in mind what I told you earlier. Over-severe calorie restriction can push the panic button on your body's metabolism (BMR) and your body processes will slow down and the fat percentage, rather than become lower, may actually stay the same.

I should add here that I have known a few bodybuilders who could rip up their physiques with just a couple of weeks of dieting, but most need a good 8–12 weeks and sometimes more.

Remember then to start your diet moderately. Begin by trimming just 200 calories from your regular daily intake for a week, then drop a further 100 calories every two or three days, until the proper level is reached.

The following is a typical low-calorie but nutritious pre-contest diet. The size of the portions you consume are dependent on your individual calorie requirements.

Rachel McLish works her thigh biceps.

Ulf Larsen of Sweden.

Sample Pre-contest Diet

Breakfast
mixed fresh fruit with sprinkling of bran or oatmeal
egg whites
coffee, tea or water (no sugar)

Lunch
broiled fish (sole, halibut)
spinach or dark green vegetables
baked potato (no butter or sour cream)
one piece fresh fruit
coffee, tea, or water (no sugar)

Dinner
broiled chicken white meat or turkey breast (remove skin before cooking)
brown rice
light salad (no dressing, only lemon juice)
coffee, tea, or water (no sugar)

Snacks
raw vegetables such as carrots, celery, radishes

With this type of diet you will notice a significant reduction in body-fat levels. You may even feel that you are losing too much muscle mass. If this is the case, you will have to moderately increase your food intake: eat more, but *never* eat so much at one meal that you are stuffed. *Never* resort to eating junk foods.

If you are not losing fast enough reduce your overall calorie content even more. But generally speaking, one's overall calorie consumption shouldn't go too low, as in a crash diet. Why not go lower? Because, as I indicated earlier, there is a likelihood of the body "shutting down" its metabolic rate. It's better to increase aerobic activity and do stationary bike riding rather then to reduce calorie levels too drastically.

Bev Francis performs the concentration curl: start *finish*

3 Months and Counting: Pre-Contest Training

Depending on how good your condition is, a pre-contest training routine should be started 10–20 weeks in advance of a contest date. Most bodybuilders begin 12 weeks out from the contest date.

There is no such thing as the perfect pre-contest routine. Everyone's routine is slightly different, and may change from workout to workout. Some people will prefer one type of routine while others will lean towards an entirely different set-up, depending on the body parts they need to get into shape. Several of the most popular pre-contest training methods have already been described.

In addition to gradually tightening your calorie intake, you should intensify your training and add extra exercises during the countdown period. Make a concerted effort to reduce the rest time between sets, with a goal of no more than 20–30 seconds between sets. Supersets are very much suited to a ripped-up rou-

Germany's Jusup Wilcosz concentrates on preacher bench dumbbell curls.

Larry Scott works his triceps at World Gym with a dumbbell triceps stretch.

Bent-over lateral raises are a favorite rear deltoid exercise for Ali Mala.

tine, so try to use them in part of the routine. Use peak contraction, isotension, and continuous-tension reps wherever possible. Increase the amount of aerobic exercise.

The Pre-Contest Routine presented here is from my book *Reps!* (Sterling Publishing Co. Inc., New York). It is one of the most popular pre-contest routines and works the entire body. In it you will notice many isolation exercises. This is necessary to bring out separation and cuts distinguishing one muscle from another. Use dumbbells and cables in preference to barbells for the same reason. Use all the principles for adding intensity that were discussed. Each body part should be worked three times a week instead of twice a week as is normal during off-season training.

1

2

3

4

John Cardillo works at the seated cable row movement.

Pre-Contest Routine

Chest	Sets		Reps
Bench Press	5	×	8–10
Incline Dumbbell Bench Press	5	×	8–10
Flat Bench Flye	4	×	10
Cable Crossover	4	×	10

Shoulders			
Seated Dumbbell Press	5	×	8
Seated Dumbbell Lateral Raise	4	×	10
Bent-over Lateral Raise	4	×	12
Alternate Forward Dumbbell Raise	4	×	12

Thighs			
Hack Lift	5	×	10
Thigh Extension	5	×	10–15
Lunge	4	×	12
Thigh Curl	5	×	10–12

Calves			
Standing Calf Raise	4	×	15–20
Seated Calf Raise	4	×	15
Donkey Calf Raise	4	×	15–25

Back			
Wide-grip Cable Pull-down behind Neck	4	×	10
Pulldown to Chest	4	×	12
Single-arm Dumbbell Row	4	×	10
Seated Cable Row	4	×	12
Hyperextension	4	×	10–15

Biceps	Sets		Reps
Incline Dumbbell Curl	4	×	10
Preacher Bench Dumbbell Curl (90 degrees)	4	×	8–10
Lying Dumbbell Curl	4	×	10
Seated Concentration Curl	4	×	12

Triceps			
Seated Dumbbell Triceps Stretch	4	×	10
Cradle Bench Pulley (face down)	4	×	10
Triceps Pressdown	4	×	10–12
Bent-over Dumbbell Kickback	4	×	8–10

Abdominals			
Broomstick Twist	3	×	200
Hanging Knee Raise	3	×	20
Crunch	3	×	20
Lying Half Sit-up	3	×	15

Forearms			
Reverse Curl	5	×	10–12
Wrist Curl	5	×	10

Thigh extensions build cuts into the thighs. Anja Langer demonstrates.

1

2

3

2 Weeks and Counting: Preventing Water Retention

Water retention can be a problem for contestants. For the muscles to look good, they have to contain plenty of water—the normal percentage is about 70 percent. But whereas water is needed *in* the muscle cells, it is not desirable to have water in the subcutaneous area between the skin and the muscle. When there is water under the skin, the body looks puffy. There are no deep cuts separating one muscle from another. The system is waterlogged and unimpressive.

One of the side effects of steroid use is that those drugs cause a water-retention problem, especially oral steroids. Lesser known causes of water retention are:

- Overtraining
- Sodium (salt)
- Stress
- Excessive carbohydrate or water intake
- Air travel and changing time zones

Overtraining

Training hard and aggressively right up to the day of a contest you are entering is not advisable. It is far better to do some stationary bike riding and posing during the last three or four days. Make a point of *not* doing heavy abdominal work the last week. Heavy-duty training, especially if prolonged over several hours at a time, causes edema (swelling) and your muscles will flatten out just when you want them to pop out.

Sodium

The dreaded salt—it's everywhere! Sodium has a powerful influence on

John Cardillo works his deltoids.

Mohamed Makkawy works on the seated calf raise.

water in the body because *one part sodium holds 180 parts water*. While potassium from potassium chloride (salt) tends to concentrate inside the cell, the sodium accumulates outside the cell, and acts to pull water from the muscle cell into the space between the cells. This produces the puffy appearance that smooths out definition and causes the body to appear flat or even bloated.

Sodium deficiencies are rare because the recommended daily requirement is low. Most people eat far too much salt, the average consumption being almost two teaspoons of salt (5,000 to 10,000 milligrams) per day. For example, the average hamburger with fixings contains 1,510 milligrams of sodium, while a fast-food fried chicken dinner with three pieces of chicken has 2,125 milligrams. That's why you shouldn't use table salt. Avoid pickled foods. Before contest time you should only eat those foods that have the absolute minimum of sodium content listed on p. 103.

Stress

Ask Samir Bannout about water retention and stress. He'll tell you that stress was one of the culprits that prevented him from peaking at numerous shows right up until the London Olympia, a show at which he turned up ripped to the bone. Samir's water problem was becoming almost a standing joke, but when he cut back on his sodium intake, increased his potassium supplementation

Scott Wilson and Ed Kawak on stage.

Aaron Baker works at the seated row movement as Laura Beaudry watches.

John Hnatyschak goes for biceps development with the barbell curl.

and learned not to allow excessive stress into his life, especially when a contest was pending, the laughter from the competition turned into dismay. Once he had solved his problem Samir became virtually unbeatable.

Excessive Carbohydrate or Water Intake

Carbohydrate is stored in the muscles as glycogen. When we train we deplete glycogen levels. By eating carbohydrates we replenish them, but we have to eat the right amount, not too little and not too much. Each gram of carbohydrate stored in the muscles as glycogen holds three grams of water. This situation has its benefits: water-suffused muscles look great. But if we eat more carbohydrate than we need for energy and cell replenishment, the water in the muscles spills over into the area between muscles and skin.

Water *is* needed for muscle bulk, but there is a consumption limit past which we must not go. Without water our muscles will look flat. With too much we will have body-bloat. Once again, not too little and not too much.

Rick Valente and James DeMelo hit chest poses in Gold's foyer.

Lee Haney backstage.

Air Travel and Changing Time Zones

Air travel can adversely affect your water retention. Ask Matt Mendenhall, who had more seminars as an amateur than most pros. Matt spends weekend after weekend doing guest appearances and seminars all over the world. He has crossed time zones more frequently than most people cross their legs! Changing time zones affects the body's circadian rhythm and thus hormone production. The effect was that his system reacted by holding water. He could never fully rip up.

More and more today people who fly in to important contests are arriving up to a week ahead of the event. They want to acclimatize to the new time zone and allow their bodies the luxury of doing without stressful air travel during the day prior to competing. I should add that not all bodybuilders find air travel contributes to waterlogging the body. But there are a significant number who swear that it does.

One Week and Counting

The last days prior to your competition are the most crucial. This is make or break time. Nerves are frayed. Hunger pangs abound. Pre-contest nerves may become evident and energy levels can drop. It's an anxious time for the bodybuilder.

A week prior to competition cut out all sodium (salt) from the diet to avoid water retention. Surprisingly, you'll find sodium in many seemingly innocent foods. Soda water or seltzer is one. Others include spinach, broccoli, brussels sprouts, cabbage, carrots, chard

Rich Gaspari and John Hnatyschak wait out those final pre-contest moments backstage.

(very high), milk, yogurt, beef, lamb, pork, chicken, turkey, pink salmon, scallops, canned salmon (very high), watercress, turnips, shrimp, whitefish, tomato, parsley, wheat germ, whole wheat bread, cottage cheese (very high), ocean perch, oats, sunflower seeds and brown rice.

Those foods that have no sodium or only the slightest trace include: Fresh yellow corn, hot green peppers, sweet red peppers, lime juice, vinegar, brook trout, lake trout, crab meat, octopus, safflower oil, unsalted butter, artificial sweeteners, dark buckwheat flour and green bulb onions.

Don't eat airline or restaurant foods since you can't "check labels," but if you absolutely *have* to eat at a hotel or restaurant then have a special talk with the chef. Explain that you *absolutely must not have any salt*. Tell him your very life depends on it. He may be able to find some of the just-mentioned foods for you. Plain baked potatoes, sweet potatoes or squash are also ideal pre-contest foods. A good rule is, "If you don't know the sodium content, don't eat it!" This advice even applies to water. During the last week you should drink *only* distilled water.

Joe Bucci, Mr. World.

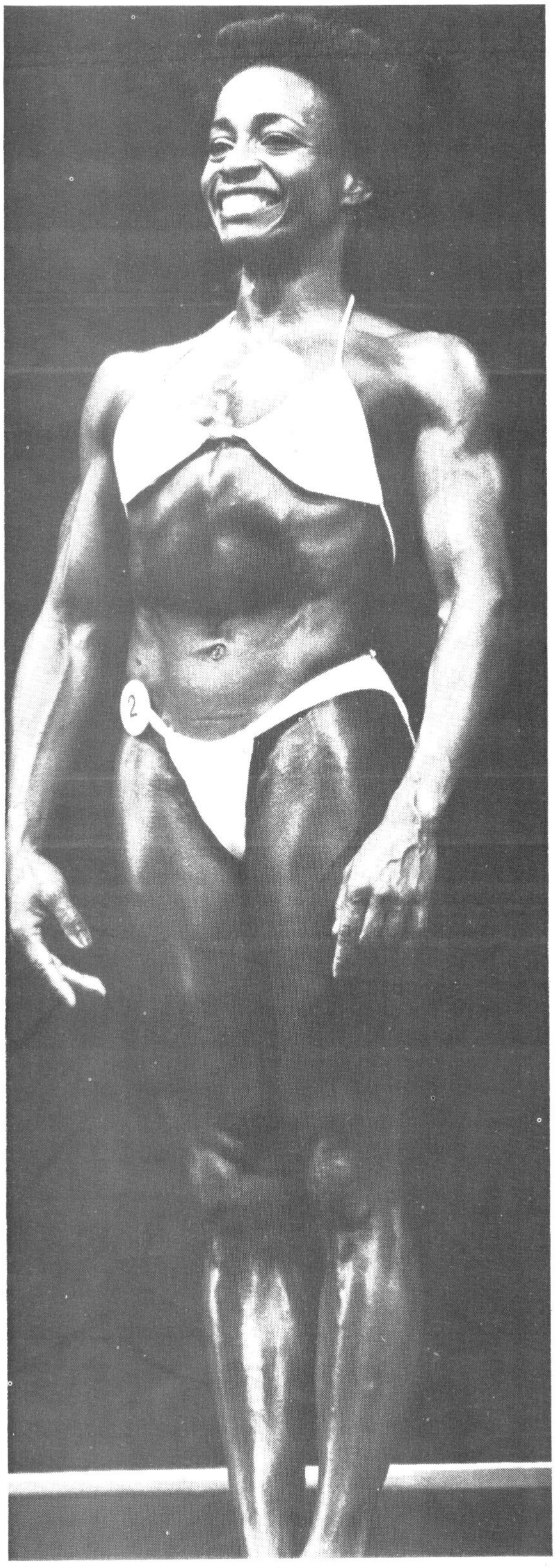

Carla Dunlap

Britain's Brian Buchannan.

How much water should you drink? The proper path is the *middle* path. Consume enough water to keep the muscles full, yet not so much that the water in the muscles spills over into the subcutaneous area under the skin, bringing about the dreaded bloated appearance that has been the downfall of so many bodybuilding hopefuls.

Potassium Supplements

Potassium is a mineral that helps you balance the water in muscle and

Gary Strydom gets into the action of wide grip pulldowns to widen his back.

1

2

3

minimizes its occurrence beneath the skin. Potassium supplementation is important during the last three pre-contest days. This supplementation should be coordinated with a low-sodium intake. No one can tell you exactly what dosage of potassium is best, but the usual recommendation is for 100 milligrams five times daily (total 500 milligrams) for a 200-pound bodybuilder. Always take potassium supplements with meals, never on an empty stomach.

Carb Loading

Most successful bodybuilders (though not all) use an important trick of the trade to maximize their cuts and mass on the day of the competition. Bill Dobbins, a writer and photographer for *Flex* and *Muscle and Fitness* magazines, was the first to fully document and describe this preparatory method, an accepted technique that many advanced bodybuilders often loosely refer to as "carbing up." The method was first used by runners to give them added energy on the day of competition, then developed by Swedish physiologist Eric Hultman as a method to concentrate more carbohydrate (as glycogen) in the muscle tissue than normal.

Start approximately one week to ten days before the show. To follow this system you engage in a low-carbohydrate diet for four to six days in order to deplete carbohydrate stores. This is very tough. The body will crave carbohydrates. You may lose your focus and even your resolve to continue. It is very hard on the body especially when one has to train at the same time. Your physique can become flat looking and you may even become depressed. A few pros eat only

Bob Paris

Ian Dowe of Britain.

30 grams of carbohydrate daily at this time, for 1–3 days.

After this low-carb phase, you "load up" with complex carbohydrates such as bread or pasta during the last 3 or 4 days immediately preceding the contest date. As a result, your muscles will appear full and cut, and your vascularity will be prominent. Take in small quantities of carbohydrates every two or three hours during working hours. The usual intake would not exceed 1½ grams per pound of body weight per day during this carb-loading period. Eat complex carbohydrates only: simple carbohydrates such as ice cream, sugar, candy bars or other sugary junk foods get into the bloodstream too quickly and cause excessive fluctuations in blood sugar levels. Complex carbohydrates give you a more sustained blood sugar source.

Lee Haney performs an impromptu most muscular.

Triceps pressdowns by Gary Strydom.

Superstar Francis Benfatto of France.

You will find that the carbing-up period at the end of your carbohydrate depletion stage will work almost miraculously. Water will be driven from under your skin and pushed into the muscle cells. Your muscles will suck up the carbohydrate and water like a vacuum and because of the earlier deprivation, will overcompensate and store 4 to 5 grams of glycogen per 100 grams of muscle weight instead of the more usual 2 to 3 grams per 100 grams of muscle weight. During those final days you will become bigger, harder and more ripped.

Never eat big meals when carbing up. Your muscles can only accept so much at any one time. Bill Dobbins suggests a minimum of 25 grams of carbohydrate per hour per day, which is equivalent to an average baked potato or two small oranges. Ideal carbing-up foods include corn, fruits, whole wheat bread, pasta, raw green vegetables, and wild rice.

While at the carbing stage (the last three days) drink moderate amounts of *distilled* water. Do not take diuretics to get rid of water or try to dehydrate the body. Allow yourself moderate amounts of protein and small amounts of fat. You can eat some lean beef or egg yolk at this stage, but only if you have done your early dieting properly (i.e.: you should be slightly below your best contest weight a week *before* the carbing-up phase).

Needless to say, you should run through this for practice before the contest, perhaps even several times. Find out when you peak, and for how long. Even the pros have been known to miscalculate on this crucial step. Build on what you have learned from one contest to the next.

One book I love to read and re-read is Clarence Bass's *Ripped* 2. He self-publishes this little gem and it is advertised in the various bodybuilding magazines. Get a copy for your home library. Bass writes in a very simple way, but the beauty of his material is that it is totally honest beyond all doubt. He relates back to various contests he's entered, and then proceeds to explain how he trained and dieted for each, and he does it all in minute detail. He's a joy to read because that's what aspiring bodybuilders want: specific details and concise instruction with complete honesty.

Britain's Frank Richards.

Barbell shrugs build the traps: Ali Mala shows how.

Joseph Grolmus of West Germany.

Pre-Contest Training: The Week of the Show

The last week prior to competing, continue to train up to the Wednesday prior to the Saturday night competition. A few successful bodybuilders do train right up to the competition while others make the Monday workout their last, a full five days before the event. The idea behind not training the last few days is that heavy weight training causes a degree of edema or swelling, but after a three-day layoff this edema usually vanishes, and you achieve a more rugged, cut appearance.

Steve Davis

Timing is Crucial

Many bodybuilders have failed to rip up for a planned contest due to mistakes in timing or judgment. First, it is very difficult to tell by looking at yourself in the mirror whether you are shredded, super-ripped, ripped or merely in good shape. Most bodybuilders have to rely on close friends to tell them whether they are "ready" or not. I couldn't begin to count the times when name bodybuilders have come up to me before a show telling me that they are cut-to-ribbons and are sure to blow everyone else off the stage, when it wasn't so. Conversely, it's not unusual for a bodybuilder to be totally cut and *not* realize it. For example, back in 1977 I sponsored a young Steve Davis to compete in London, England at the NABBA Mr. Universe show. Backstage he told me that he was in pretty good shape, but in reality when he got on stage it was obvious that he was the most ripped man in the contest. Not big enough to win, but nevertheless, very impressive. Later at other contests Steve would tell me that he was "cut to the bone," but he never approached that NABBA condition again.

"I should look OK," said Marjo Selin before the Ms. Olympia 1987 contest in New York. Her face was lean and there was hunger in her eyes. "At least I feel pretty good. I just hope I don't look bad!" When she stepped out on stage Marjo was so cut that a razor blade wouldn't have been competition. The night before the same show Cathy Palyo had told me that she was "totally cut." I did manage a poke at her thigh which almost rewarded me with a broken index finger. "Strap yourself into your seat, Bob," enthused Ms. Palyo. "I'm gonna blow everyone

Marjo Selin

Cathy Palyo

away." On stage that night Cathy was a disappointment. Yes, she was hard, but the ripped and cut look was nonexistent. Curiously, a few months later at Arnold Schwarzenegger's Professional Women's World Championships in Columbus, Ohio, Ms. Palyo redeemed herself. With no night-before promises of her intentions she went on stage at the Veteran's Memorial Auditorium and did indeed

Steve Brisbois—Mr. Universe.

blow everyone away. She snatched first place from among a field of twenty women and was ripped to the bone.

Canada's Steve Brisbois got so ripped for his attempt at the IFBB World Championships event in Tokyo 1986 that he startled some of judges panel. Yet, when he entered the Mr. Olympia contest in Gothenburg, Sweden, the following year he was only a shadow of his

Renee Casella of California.

former self. I was at both contests and can testify that Brisbois made only slight miscalculations to effect such a vast difference in appearance and it was not due to a lack of hard work and effort.

Let no one say that getting contest-perfect is easy. It is an art. Even top competitors have trouble with timing. Everyone has to put several contests and some disappointing results behind them before they know how their body reacts and what regimen gets the best results for them. Once you have found what works best for you, stick with it. Don't experiment before an important contest.

The contest will come when you are at your peak—cut to the bone. Have a friend grab a camera and record what is one of the toughest but most rewarding achievements in the sport of bodybuilding—being totally ripped up.

Michael Ashley

Jim Quinn displays one of the most massive bodies of the century in this most muscular pose.

Janet Graisser

Hanne Van Aken of Rotterdam, Holland.

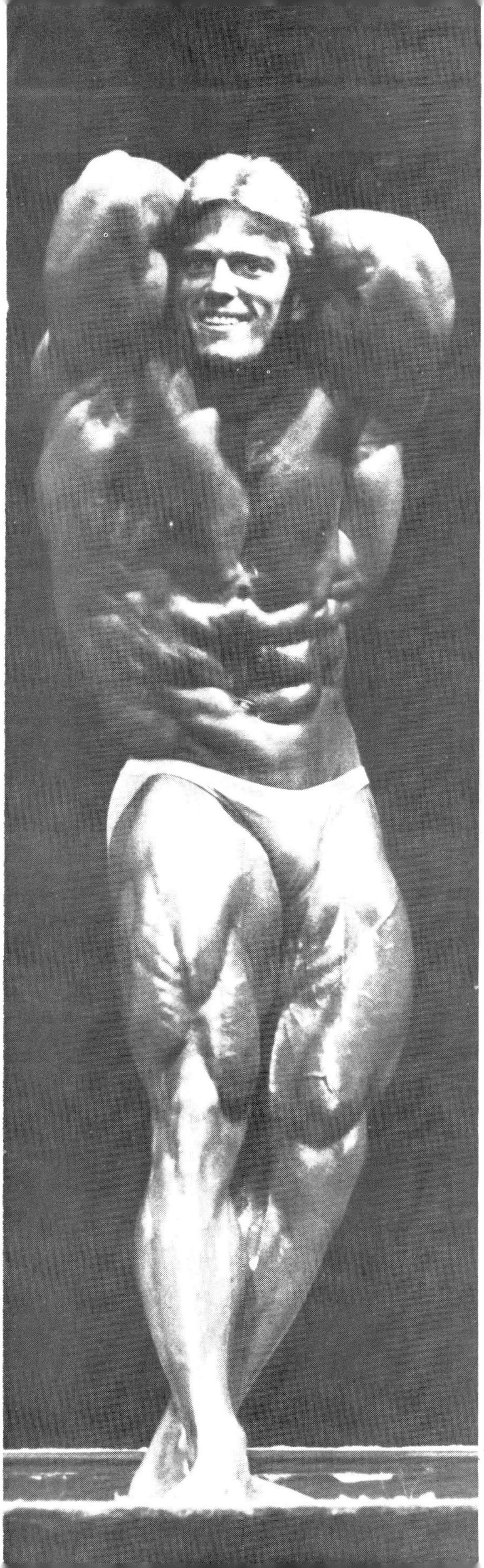
Joe Meeko

Mike Christian

Francis Benfatto of France.

Questions and Answers

Question: I have been a bodybuilder for several years now, and it always seems to me that I can only get truly ripped if I make a superhuman effort. Most of the time I am soft looking and although I am pretty well built, I have fat around my lower back and waist. Most of the guys at the gym where I train are the same. No one seems to be ripped all the time. I have seen manual laborers and men who work on construction and even pop singers who appear to be ripped. My question is: Can a person be ripped all the time?

Cory Everson

Jon Aranita

Answer: Only a small percentage of laborers are ripped; most have beer bellies. Pop singers are usually ripped because they use drugs, not because they are fit. Runners actively training for decathlons and triathlons are nearly always in super condition, but needless to say, these individuals seldom have big muscles. You may not quite be ripped, but most of us can look muscular and impressive all the time—with vigilance. Regular training is necessary and for the majority a low-fat, calorie-controlled diet is necessary, all year long. So, keep training and find a strict diet you can live with over long periods of time, one that isn't a constant strain if it's going to be year-round. Learn to like low-cal snacks like pretzel rods, unbuttered and unsalted popcorn, rice cakes, and fruit.

Question: I have heard that the bodybuilder's greatest enemy is overtraining, yet everything I read says that each workout should be harder than the next. How is a bodybuilder supposed to train harder and harder and yet not overtrain. How do I know if I'm overtraining?

Answer: Overtraining is when we train too hard, too long, or too frequently for our current physical condition. Other aspects of overtraining include training without allowing adequate rest or sufficient nutrition for full recuperation. The following are warning signs or symptoms of overtraining.

- An elevation of normal body temperature of a degree or two.
- Persistent mild soreness, stiffness and aches in the muscles, tendons or joints.
- The regular occurrence of headaches, sore throats, colds and cold sores in the mouth.
- Irritability, depression, lethargy, or anxiety with no obvious cause.
- Difficulty in sleeping or relaxing normally.
- Elevated heart rate (6–12 beats per minute elevation above normal in the morning).
- Excessive tiredness and persistent lack of energy.
- Drops in poundage used in training when there is no downward change in body weight.
- Aching stomach or queasiness, loose bowels or diarrhea.
- Loss of appetite or body weight accompanied by flat or stringy-looking muscles.

If these symptoms occur you should ease up on your training. Overtraining can be avoided by sensible training: Don't increase your weights with each successive training session, but allow several workouts until the body adjusts and the weights are easier to handle before progressing again to higher weights. Check the feedback from your body—don't progress according to an inflexible paper schedule or your ego.

Question: How good is fasting for getting a really cut body? I want to get ripped within a short period of time and it has occurred to me that going without food completely may do the trick.

Answer: Fasting is currently not in vogue. There have been times in recent history when the practice was considered healthy and "cleansing" but it is not the best way to lose fat, especially when combined with heavy workouts and strenuous aerobic activity. The reasoning is that those who fast may force their metabolic rates to shut down to conserve energy. The body will try to keep its current weight, instead of shedding pounds. Andreas Cahling, one of Sweden's greatest bodybuilders, has other ideas. He says: "The logic behind fasting is convincing." He believes that it helps the "cells rejuvenate and aids bodybuilding in general. The important thing is to start a fast slowly and go off it slowly, too." Personally I feel that fasts should only be done under medical supervision, especially when a bodybuilder is in hard training.

Question: I am anxious to look my very best for my fortieth birthday. One of my concerns, since I do carry a few extra pounds of fat on my body, is whether or not I can drink whole milk while trying to achieve a high degree of muscularity. I have always liked milk and there is no doubt that it has helped me gain mass, but now that I am trying to rip up I have second thoughts.

Answer: Milk is an excellent source of protein, fat, and carbohydrates. It contains a host of vitamins and is extremely rich in calcium for the bones. The drawbacks are as follows:

1. Lactose, a component of milk, causes an allergic reaction in many people, causing flatulence, bloating and/or diarrhea because it cannot be digested.
2. Whole milk is relatively high in fat (and fat makes you fat). Accordingly, it is not suitable for those wishing to shed subcutaneous fat from under the skin. As you say, milk has helped you gain size, but now that your goals are changing you should cut out whole milk and whole milk products such as cheese and yogurt while you are attempting to define your body. My recommendation is, assuming you are not lactose intolerant, that you gradually cut down your daily consumption of whole milk, then switch to lowfat 2 percent milk and finally drink only skim milk. More lowfat cheeses and yogurts are coming on the market. Even these may have to be limited as you lower your body-fat ratio.

Question: When I go into the gym I immediately start into bench pressing with a heavy weight and keep going until the end of the workout. Lately, people have been telling me that I should warm up first. I have *never* warmed up and neither have I ever been injured. Advice please.

Ron Love

Answer: Warming up is added health insurance. Remember you only have to injure yourself once—it could put a damper on your training for months, or even years. Many bodybuilders do not warm up. They are too keen to get into the meat and potatoes of the workout, considering warmups to be a waste of time. The truth is that warmups help avoid injury and all serious athletes should warm up before training. We have too many injured bodybuilders as it is! Warmups are a preconditioning must, especially when working with heavy weights. Their purpose is:

- to get blood circulating better
- to "oil up" your muscles and joints
- to slightly elevate heart and lung rate
- to gently stretch muscles and ligaments to prevent injury
- to ready your system for strenuous activity

Francis Benfatto dominates this IFBB Mr. Universe lineup.

Index